Mission-Driven Worship

HELPING YOUR
CHANGING CHURCH
CELEBRATE GOD

by Handt Hanson

Group
Loveland, Colorado

Group's R.E.A.L. Guarantee to you:

Every Group resource incorporates our R.E.A.L. approach to ministry— a unique philosophy that results in long-term retention and life transformation. It's ministry that's:

This is EARL.
He's R.E.A.L.
mixed up.
(Get it?)

Relational
Because student-to-student interaction enhances learning and builds Christian friendships.

Experiential
Because what students experience sticks with them up to 9 times longer than what they simply hear or read.

Applicable
Because the aim of Christian education is to be both hearers and doers of the Word.

Learner-based
Because students learn more and retain it longer when the process is designed according to how they learn best.

Credits
Author: Handt Hanson
Editor: Gary Wilde
Creative Development Editor: Paul Woods
Chief Creative Officer: Joani Schultz
Copy Editor: Janis Sampson
Art Director: Jean Bruns
Computer Graphic Artist: Tracy K. Donaldson
Illustrator: Matt Wood
Cover Art Director: Jeff A. Storm
Production Manager: Peggy Naylor

Unless otherwise noted, Scripture taken from the HOLY BIBLE, NEW INTERNATIONAL VERSION®. Copyright © 1973, 1978, 1984 by International Bible Society. Used by permission of Zondervan Publishing House. All rights reserved.

ISBN 0-7644-2347-9

Printed in the United States of America.

10 9 8 7 6 5 4 3 2 1   10 09 08 07 06 05 04 03 02 01

CONTENTS

Changing Church in a Changing World

When I was born in 1950 on a small farm outside of Milton, North Dakota, we had no electricity. We burned coal for heat in a small stove at the center of the house. We used an outdoor "facility" that stood a cold fifty-foot trek from the back door. And the first television came to our town in 1957. Talk about change in the wonderful world of technology!

But I've experienced a lot of personal change too, as I know you have. My heart and soul was formed in the hard, wooden pews of a small Lutheran church in North Dakota. Today I lead worship, music, and arts ministries for Prince of Peace, a congregation of ten thousand in a Minneapolis suburb. The delightful challenge for me in this book, then, has been to balance what I know of big-congregation-suburban church life with the realities of churches everywhere.

So with one foot in "ancient" rural North Dakota and the other firmly planted in my modern metropolitan suburb, I'm inviting you to check out the idea of mission-driven worship. On one level, it's simply a call to the great adventure of change. But it's the kind of change that I firmly believe will bring great glory to our God.

Surprisingly, in the midst of all this talk of change, you'll see that I'm actually speaking to what is common among us: our love for the Lord. To this end, I'll show you numerous practical strategies and techniques that any church can quickly begin to implement. In the process, we'll be proclaiming the "old, old story" amidst the vast new changes of our world.

Of course, so much change has already occurred in "how we do church" these days. And you don't need me to tell you that incredible changes loom on the horizon. Are you ready?

Change: It's a Good Thing!

I want to stress that whether a church is large or small is practically irrelevant. What matters is the degree of passion, intentionality, and creativity given to worship planning. This became crystal clear to me way back in 1970.

At that time a fresh wind was blowing through the campus of Concordia College in Moorhead, Minnesota. The wind roared from the west, blowing right out of California with the sounds of the "Jesus movement," marrying rock-and-roll with a radical new Christ-centered music. People our age were fed up with what seemed to be a cold, institutional church. But we were very much in love with the passion and purpose of this movement.

In 1964 when the Beatles stepped off their plane in New York City, the entire American landscape changed forever. So did the musical preferences of an entire generation. How logical that this music could also be used to express spiritual values and offer praise to God! It could hardly be ignored and, better yet, seemed to be the perfect vehicle for communicating the gospel message in a brand-new era.

We're entering another new era right now.

Yes, I believe we have come to a watershed moment in the history of the church. It's a time in which the passions that fueled the creativity of the past decades can be focused more clearly. We're now able to grasp a deeper insight into what will most benefit the church at large. And as we take up the new, life-transforming forms of ministry and worship, we'll be ensuring that the work we do today will continue to enrich the church of the future.

The burning question is this: Will we be terrorized by change, or will we joyfully embrace it as our friend? In either case, there's a deep, underlying issue. Carol Childress, of Leadership Network, puts it this way; "It's not change that's killing us, it's the transitions."

I think she's right. It's the transitions from one form to another that can be so difficult. I want those transitions to be as smooth and painless for you as they can possibly be. It's why I wrote this book.

After all, change is our permanent ongoing reality. In every moment of every day we're asked to make transitions from one form to another. And the rate of change is logarithmic. Transition time is shorter and shorter.

But remember: All change is in God's hands.

> *"For surely I know the plans I have for you, says the Lord, plans for your welfare and not for harm, to give you a future with hope. Then when you call upon me and come and pray to me, I will hear you. When you search for me, you will find me; if you seek me with all your heart, I will let you find me, says the Lord"* (JEREMIAH 29:11-14A, NEW REVISED STANDARD VERSION).

We can rest confidently in God's promises because God is good and has our best at heart. So let us welcome God's plans for the church. With God's blessing, let's resolve to make our worship times into a glorious glimpse of heaven on earth, week after week.

—Handt Hanson

CHAPTER 1

Forming a Worship Strategy

Renewing worship doesn't have to be a fight. Really! Yes, I admit that when we wade into the waters of change, we may discover that the attitudes of some church members can be rigid at best and belligerent at worst. We'll definitely encounter some strong opinions on both ends of a very broad spectrum. It can feel like struggling to keep our heads above the surface.

But there are ways to get almost everyone on board.

Start With a Plan

Let's begin with some essential, global themes that can form a basis for mutual understanding. And let's plan to get everyone on board in understanding these themes and at least assenting to the praiseworthy motives behind them. I'll present them here as important guidelines for churches to cling to as they move ahead into new forms of worship.

GUIDELINE 1:
Remember that community precedes strategy.

In his book *A Grain of Wheat,* Chuck Lofy shows that in order to move forward with a new strategy, a church must first establish authentic community among a critical mass of its leadership. Your first action in the strategic planning process is to create a safe environment, gather people in groups of ten to twelve, and get them talking honestly and openly about the central issues in your congregation.

Create groups of people who will think not only about issues of faith, but will explore what those issues mean for your congregation's future, and then will move on to form a picture of where God is leading. As authentic community begins to develop, a strategy will emerge.

In the periodical Leader to Leader (Winter 2000), Christopher Bartlett describes three movements in the business community that parallel this principle in church life:

- Moving beyond strategy to purpose. **Strategy** is "the means for allocating scarce capital resources across competing needs." **Purpose** focuses an organization on how to "attract, excite, engage, motivate, and retain people who want to do more than just work for a company." *Can the church learn this lesson as well?*

- Moving beyond structure to process. **Structure** implies the leadership of a "loyal implementor" who enforces existing orders, policies, and procedures. It focuses on a hierarchy of tasks and responsibilities. **Process** recognizes a new dynamic world and builds an organization around flexible roles and relationships. *What can the church learn from this?*

- Moving beyond systems to people. **Systems** typically focus on finances and measurable results. A **people** focus makes the "recruitment, development, motivation, engagement, and retention" of great people the core task of any leader. *Doesn't this apply to the church as well?*

We can learn from these principles. As a Christian church, we are called to build community, but in a much more profound way than as a mere business technique. Our community is based upon the reality of Christ-in-us and the work he has done for us through his birth, death, and resurrection. In short, we are bound together by a spiritual communion. Surely we ought to express this inward mystery by outward actions in our worship life together.

What does community have to do with worship? It is central. Our first call is not to establish large music programs, drama departments, or dynamic preachers; but rather to build Christian community within each of the systems that support worship. Ministry teams, worship teams, choirs, ensembles, and drama groups must all function from the foundation of Christian community. Yet we may, through hard work in building community, end up with a terrific music program as an added benefit.

GUIDELINE 2:
Think cellular!

Many churches continue to act as if a departmentalized, structured, hierarchical model will lead the church to where it needs to be. In other words, they base their life on organization.

Much has been written regarding organizational business models, and we know that not all of it applies to the church. To me, two things are clear: (1) small churches tend to be more highly organized than large churches, and (2) smaller churches might think that larger churches tend to be highly organized—and that this is what leads to their perceived "success."

Our experience leads me to believe that quite the opposite is true. Larger churches tend to be in such constant transition that organizational systems quickly implode upon one another. Larger churches that recognize the organic (not organizational) nature of the church have a glimpse of where the church is headed, and their organic nonstructures provide a creative environment in which the work of the church can continue to develop and grow.

An organism is made up of cells. It is a living, breathing, changing entity whose realities differ at any given moment because of changes in the environment. Dr. Carl George has written extensively on this "meta-church" model and the nature of cellular development. The cell (a small group) is the basis of all dynamic church life. That life is what we need to feed. In feeding the cells, we feed the organism.

A "cell group" could be a group of four to twelve individuals in dynamic discussion about their common or uncommon concerns.

These folks get to know each other, love each other, pray and read Scripture together, and serve in ministry together. If every aspect of church ministry (from the facilities team to the church council) behaved like a cell, the church would be truly alive.

So don't attempt to build an organization; rather, nurture an organism. In order to "think big," the church must also be able to "think small." Feed the cells. Be organized, but organize yourselves strategically around the living organism called the church.

GUIDELINE 3:
Keep functioning as a learning life-form.

I've said that the church should be viewed as an organism, and I want to add to that. I would propose that the church is really a *learning* organism. Peter Senge, in his book *The Fifth Discipline*, introduces the theory of a learning organization. The church has typically viewed itself as a teaching organization. Certainly important truths must be taught; but we should never lose sight of our commitment to learning, not just as individuals, but as the large organism called the church. The point is that just because a thing is taught does not mean it has been learned.

Are we willing to invest in reinventing ourselves for learning? Worship should fit into a whole process of doing ministry, a process that integrates the efforts of all areas of work and every outreaching effort. The feedback that comes through all of these efforts is the best learning tool of all! As we learn, we adjust for greater effectiveness and increased effort.

And so a dynamic cycle of learning unfolds.

To summarize: The church is a living, breathing entity whose foundation of life is the cell (community). This entity needs to begin to view itself as a learning organism where every minute of every day is an opportunity to reshape and reinvent itself as the fluid realities of life confront it. It grows and flourishes as its various members exercise their ministries for mutual edification. It's really nothing new, since it's the picture of the church the Apostle Paul gave to us centuries ago:

> *"The gifts he gave were that some would be apostles, some prophets, some evangelists, some pastors and teachers, to equip the saints for the work of ministry, for building up the body of Christ, until all of us come to the unity of the faith and of the knowledge of the Son of God, to maturity, to the measure of the full stature of Christ"* (EPHESIANS 4:11-13, NRSV).

This church organism is adaptable, changeable, flexible, innovative, creative, caring, inventive, intentional, and focused. All of this, and more! In fact, if we look closely we see some pretty unique qualities in such a church.

- It focuses on the spiritual welfare of the individual, and this focus shapes its global vision and mission.
- It simultaneously directs attention to the biggest and smallest of questions. It is able to consider global concerns and individual needs at the same time.
- It is flexible enough to adapt its vision and mission to changing cultural and environmental demands.
- It is creative enough to establish a unique identity rather than just duplicating the ministry of another congregation.
- It is inventive enough to identify particular ministry needs at its back door and turn them into front-door possibilities.
- It lets hard questions become opportunities for rethinking and re-forming through its organic, lifelong system of learning.

Are you beginning to see what all of this has to do with worship? If we simply create worship services that are unrelated to our organic existence as a complete system, that is exactly what our services will continue to be: *unrelated.* We'll continue to have worship that is mostly irrelevant, stagnant, lacking real-life application, and...boring.

Accomplish Your Objective

All I'm saying is that worship must be a living, organic learning environment in order for the beliefs, values, mission, and vision of a congregation to flourish. And everything I've said above will help bring you inevitably to your goal: vision-led, mission-driven worship in your church. The congregation of the future will have a good grasp of its vision and mission, which will illuminate its future.

What we're really doing is building a house of worship that brings glory to God. Let's think in terms of "building blocks," then, for the rest of this chapter. Eventually the whole process will seem less like a war than an exciting construction project. What are these building blocks to healthy, organic, learning-rich worship renewal? Here they are, starting at the foundation and moving upward.

Beliefs. A church builds its vision on the beliefs that formed and shaped it. For each church these beliefs are directly related to its theology, doctrine, and practice.

Values. A church builds its values on the beliefs its members share in common. Values tend to emerge out of genuine community and are commonly held attitudes and behaviors that are accepted and appreciated.

Mission. A church's mission emerges from its beliefs and values and is a statement of what it can accomplish as the members work together. It often includes a description of *how* the mission will be accomplished.

Vision. According to George Barna, a vision is "a clear mental image of a preferable future imparted by God to His chosen servants, and is based upon an accurate understanding of God, self and circumstances."[1] A vision is your church's preferred future, a thing that is so large and unattainable that only God could make it happen. It's possible to confuse vision and mission. Vision paints a picture of your preferred future. Mission is a broad, general, philosophical statement that depicts the heart of the ministry and how you will do your work together to accomplish the vision.

Outcomes. After all is said and done (and usually more is said than done!), these are the specific behaviors, disciplines, and attitudes you are hoping will be evident in the life of those affiliated with your congregation.

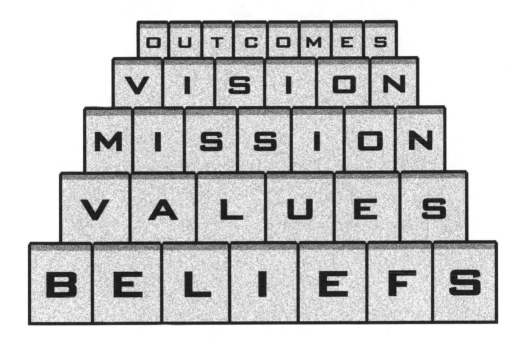

How It Works Where I Work!

To illustrate, let me close this chapter by listing some of the specific building blocks we use at Prince of Peace. Perhaps they will stimulate your thinking about what will work best in your own church.

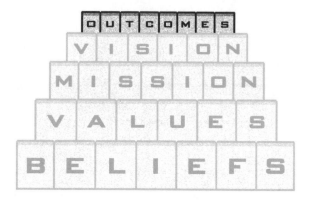

"The Marks of Discipleship" at our church:

Pray daily (1 Thessalonians 5:16-19)

Worship weekly (Psalm 122:1; Hebrews 10:23-25)

Read the Bible (Psalm 119:105)

Serve in ministry (1 Corinthians 12:4-13; Matthew 25:31-46)

Relationships for spiritual growth (Mark 6:7; Romans 15:1-6)

Give of time, talent, and treasure (Malachi 3:10; 2 Corinthians 8:12)

To help our community easily remember the Marks of Discipleship, we label these outcomes as **PoWeR SuRGe**.

Ten thousand passionate followers of Jesus Christ in every generation

Prince of Peace Church exists to
 Welcome people to faith in Jesus Christ
 Equip people with a faith that works in real life
 Send people into the world to serve in Jesus' name

At Prince of Peace, we value
 Growing faith in Jesus Christ Community
 Personal integrity   Innovation
 Respect for others   Excellence

At Prince of Peace, we believe in
> The Word of God
> The historic Christian creeds
> Our denominational confessions

Do you like how it looks? It will come out differently in your own congregation, but the basic principles of building an organic, learning community are universally applicable. I invite you to try them on for size and begin the journey toward mission-driven worship as soon as you can.

CHECKPOINTS

1. Is your church focused primarily on being an *organization* or an *organism*? How do you know? What examples can you cite?
2. What things would change in your church if it became more focused on purpose, process, and people?
3. To what extent does each group, choir, and ensemble work at relationship-building as part of its process of accomplishing its tasks? What would happen if, every time they met, the people in these groups learned more about each other, prayed together, read Scripture together, and discussed their ideas and feelings?
4. What practical things could your church begin doing to feed and nurture the life and health of all its "cells"?

SUMMARY POINTS

1. We are called to transition through change for God's purposes to be fulfilled.

2. Building Christian community is our central call, and it precedes strategy.

3. The church is a living organism not unlike a cell. In order to think "big," the church must also think "small."

4. The church is a learning organism that continually rethinks and reinvests its energies.

5. The church is a learning organism that is able to adapt, change, innovate, create, care, invent, and focus in order to move into God's future.

6. Worship is founded on the beliefs that form and shape the church.

7. Worship is a gathering of God's people who agree to a set of shared core values.

8. Worship is a place where the church's mission and vision are shared and understood.

9. Worship is an environment where the marks of discipleship are learned and experienced.

10. Worship is one of many settings where the people of God take action steps to accomplish the mission that God has for us.

Notes: Chapter 1

1. George Barna, *The Power of Vision* (Ventura, CA: Regal Books, 1992), 28.

CHAPTER 2

Ship-Shaping Your Worship

According to a recent Barna survey, "92 percent of all churched adults…said that it is very important to them to worship God."[1] This desire to worship is encouraging, however many of our churches are not providing an experience of God's presence in worship. Another Barna study revealed that only "one-third of church attenders said they always feel they experience God's presence or interact with Him at church."[2] What can we do to help people in our churches experience God's presence in worship?

Worship is not only the most visible program a church offers, it deserves all the time, money, attention, and detailed planning necessary to make it compelling and meaningful. While most congregations would agree with this premise, lots of worship leaders continue to just plug in new hymn numbers and call it worship planning.

So what do we do? In our ongoing attempt to clearly define our task (begun in the previous chapter), we need to develop a philosophy of worship. We need to agree on a few important matters: (1) the basic characteristics of good worship, (2) some general requirements for renewed worship, (3) the practical nuts and bolts of worship scheduling, and (4) the overall "look" of an effective worship structure. Finally, to close out this chapter, I'll offer some practical do's and don'ts to keep in mind as you seek to remove the "drag" from the rudder of this ship we call wor*ship*.

Characterizing a Worship That Works

Most basically, worship is what gives theological structure to the rest of the church organism. You see, culture-setting happens in worship. When we come to worship, we are proclaiming the essentials about us. We gather as sinful people in need of a Savior, a common ground upon which every worshipper can walk. We share a common humanity, a common need, and a common hope. Our need for a Savior and the action of God on our behalf is the central story of worship. It is the central story of the church, the theological structure of the people we call our community. When we share Scripture, songs, the creeds, the Lord's Prayer, we join together in a common understanding of our need and our hope.

Yet worship is primarily about what God is doing. It's not, in its essence, all about what pastors or musicians are doing, although each serves to bring God's activity to light. Good worship gathers people in public space and, through Word and sacrament, directs them toward God. Essentially, God is going to show up and surprise us. Are we ready for what God has for us today? The focus isn't on the personalities or talents of anyone in a leadership role. Although good worship may have an "entertaining" means of communication, it's important for worship leaders to struggle with the fine line between entertainment and worship leadership.

Though worship is about what God is doing, it does demand active participation by God's people. The word *liturgy*, which means "work of the people," implies the active participation of all the gathered people, a wide spectrum representing folks from first-time worshipper to long-time member. To worship is to act: sing, pray, read, respond, commune, engage, interact, think, confess, receive, and share. All are action words, and a good worship plan utilizes all of them. Each individual in the congregation needs to sense that he or she is critical to the effectiveness of the worship service, far from being a mere spectator in an event led by someone else.

So worship is *God-focused* and *people-active*. This is the proper orientation for mission-driven worship in the new millennium. Worship needs to be focused on God and the things of God, yet intimately related to the needs and concerns of God's people so they can actively participate with enthusiasm and genuineness. This is a healthy and delicate tension to work out each week. But it can be done! It's clear that the era of church worship as a pop-psychology forum is over. The day of the "felt needs" preaching series has come and gone. Worship needs to grow beyond the self-help arena and into a vertical focus that informs our horizontal realities.

The vertical focus comes through especially in our highlighting of Word, prayer, and sacrament. This is the best kind of worship. Through the means of grace, God meets us in this public place of worship. The risen Christ is present in bread and wine. In water and Word we die to our sin and rise to eternal life in Christ. We are immersed in the ritual actions of Christian community, according to the unique richness of our particular denominations. Earthly elements—water, bread, and wine— are the touch of God in human time.

The focal points of Christian worship are table and bath!

To summarize: We want to be known as a church of God's Word, a church committed to prayer, and a church where symbolism and ritual are honored, taught, and experienced. Good worship planning begins, then, with God's Word. Prayer is the fabric that holds the tapestry of worship together. Sacrament is the tactile, tangible, mysterious experience of the risen Christ among us.

Recognizing the Requirements for "Quality" Worship

Now, if we're going to create an experience of the presence of God, we're going to have to meet at least three essential requirements. First, worship needs a good and faithful plan. Effective worship utilizes the best, most faithful plan the worship leaders and creative teams can create. We often approach the process backward, asking, "What are the pastors and musicians going to do today?" Instead, we need to be asking, "What will God do among us? What might God do in our midst? What will the gathered congregation be invited into? *What plan can we develop to assist that process?*" All worship is worthy of prayerful deliberation and meticulous planning.

Second, worship needs high-quality, consistent leadership. This, in turn, leads to high expectations. Quality and consistency result in long-term gains that usually ripple through the church programming. Focus your energies on quality people and great music. Make this a consistent pattern over time, and you'll discover that more and more people are choosing this worship experience as their own.

Third, worship deserves a long-term commitment. This is not a trial run or a spur-of-the-moment experiment! If you begin a new worship format with less than full commitment, you'll seriously undermine the success of the effort. If begun as a trial, it has no credibility. A commitment to a new worship option should be made for the life of your church or eternity—whichever comes first! If those who want to kill this new venture see that it's a trial run, they will have a clear time frame in which to do their damage. But if the decision has been made without time limits, there is no reason to mount an attack. The worship will evolve to whatever it can become in the space you have provided, and leadership will not have predetermined that level. You're not saying what it will become; you're making a commitment to support this emerging worship form in the life of your church.

Some fifteen years ago we began a new Saturday night worship at Prince of Peace. The first service attracted thirty-seven people, and we felt we were off to a great start. Over a year later, there were still only thirty-seven people attending that service. We were, however, committed to it, and though our intellect told us to eliminate it, our intuition told us we were doing the right thing. Somewhere between years two and four, things began to change. Now nearly five hundred people call that worship service their own. Worship deserves a commitment for the long haul.

Scheduling All Those Services!

Patterned, thematic, scriptural worship is our goal, and that requires a good amount of scheduling and structuring. How do we do it at our church? Located in a suburban setting on the south side of the Minneapolis/St. Paul Metroplex, Prince of Peace is a thirty-six-year-old congregation that draws from several communities. We consider ourselves a regional church and intentionally break down boundaries that tend to form in a "parish" setting. From a worship perspective, our experience would lead us to recommend the following principles in terms of schedule:

• All worship should be scheduled at regular times, every week, all year long.

• Don't alter your schedule weekly or monthly. It takes people about two years to adapt to any schedule change. A consistent, long-term schedule will build confidence in your intentions.

• The new worship option should never replace an existing worship service. It's a better strategy to *add* a new worship service than to eliminate or change one that already exists.

• We must provide a worship experience that compels our members to bring others to worship. New worship simply adds additional options to the weekly schedule. Newcomers will be invited by those who are confident in the consistency and quality of the worship they plan to attend.

• If you are not offering worship in "prime time," you need a schedule change. Most research shows that a first-time worshipper will expect a church to offer worship during midmorning. That same research shows that if these folks come once, and there is not a worship event for them, they will not return. Churches that offer an early worship service, then an education hour, then a late morning worship might consider this: If worship is central to congregational life, you must offer worship in prime time.

• Don't cut back your schedule in the summer; instead, offer another option specifically designed to attract visitors. You might consider implementing outdoor worship, as we did at Prince of Peace nearly thirty years ago. (We'll look more closely at this option in chapter 5.)

THE PRINCE OF PEACE SCHEDULE

Saturday at 5:30 p.m.—*The Gathering*

Sunday at 8 a.m.—*Festival Worship*

Sunday at 9 a.m. and 10:10 a.m.—*Celebration Worship*

Sunday at 9:45 a.m.—*The JYM Gathering* (Jesus, You and Me at the local YMCA)

Sunday at 11:20 a.m.—*Wide Awake!*

Some church planners say that scheduling is everything—that "where" and "when" are critical in the world of worship. You might find our worship schedule to be illuminating in several ways. The times we've chosen allow for fifty-minute Sunday services. The services all have a name, not a style designation such as "traditional" or "contemporary." The services offer a great deal of diversity while maintaining common themes, texts, and preaching.

Our worship weekend begins on Saturday at 5:30 p.m. with The Gathering, which is centered around singing uplifting music led by a worship band, practical preaching, and participating in Communion. Sunday services begin at 8 a.m. with Festival Worship, which features the great hymns and liturgy of our heritage, weekly Communion, great preaching, instrumental ensembles, soloists, and organ music. Then Celebration Worship comes at 9 a.m. (sign-language interpreted) and 10:10 a.m. It blends and fuses great hymns and songs led by the organ, choirs, instrumental ensembles, and worship bands. It combines technological communication elements with drama, art, and great preaching. Finally, Wide Awake! is the 11:20 a.m. experience. It's a more informal, spontaneous format led by a worship band together with technological communication elements and great preaching.

The JYM Gathering is an outreach worship event held at the local YMCA. It's an informal forty-five-minute service targeted toward those without a church home, offering free use of the recreational facilities following worship until noon. This event serves as a launching pad for ministries into local subsidized housing complexes and apartment buildings.

Communion is offered every week on Saturday at 5:30 p.m. and Sunday at 8 a.m. and at all services on the first weekend of each month. Baptisms take place on the third weekend of each month on Saturday at 5:30 p.m., Sunday at 11:20 a.m., and during a special service in the sanctuary at 12:30 p.m. Four times per year we hold baptisms at all services. We also hold many special-event worship experiences during the year, including

- a Martin Luther King Jr. celebration.

- first Communion events, culminating in Saturday worship.

- Lord's Prayer parties, culminating in Saturday worship.

- Bible distribution to fourth graders, culminating in Saturday worship.

- Alpha worship (fifteen minutes of worship each Monday night to kickoff the Alpha Bible study sessions).

- a Super Bowl service at noon on the last Sunday in January (a brief worship service on the same text and theme of the weekend—held outdoors in Minnesota in January!).

- an Ash Wednesday worship at noon, 5:30 p.m., and 7 p.m. (The noon service is for those unable to drive at night. The 5:30 service is for families with small children. The 7 p.m. service is led by the worship band and all services include the imposition of ashes.)

- Maundy Thursday and Good Friday services that are held at noon and 7 p.m.

- healing services that are held in the chapel six times a year.

- Thanksgiving Eve services that are held at 5:30 p.m. for families with small children and 7 p.m.

- a Service of Remembrance held one weekday evening before Christmas Eve. (It is a time for people to come and have candles lit in memory of lost loved ones. Tools for grief work are offered to those who attend.)

- a Crosswalk Worship for the first twenty minutes of each church school session.

- a Junior high worship (a thirty-minute segment of each Wednesday session).

- a Senior high worship (a twenty-minute closing of each Wednesday session).

Working Out a Working Structure

Once we have our scheduling worked out, we need to make sure that the worship experience itself has a well-planned structure. For centuries, people have gathered in public space for worship, and their gatherings have taken a patterned structure. This overall form springs not only from the archetypal nature of human beings but from a pattern in which we are accustomed to behaving in public. Worship form grows from traditional roots and focuses on Word, prayer, and sacrament. But the tension between *what was* and *what will be* is the creative space in which we find ourselves today.

First, we hold that the common, historical four-fold pattern of worship is a wise and useable place to begin worship planning:

- Entrance
- Word
- Table
- Sending

This construction serves to give order and balance to the planning of worship. The form and substance of what might happen in this pattern is the creative area in which worship planners need to make good choices for the sake of the church community.

Building on the four-fold pattern of worship, we have made slight modifications to accommodate a mindset that emerges from our particular mission statement. Since "mission" describes how we intend to be with one another, a three-fold pattern not only serves the purpose of worship construction but also reinforces the mission of our church. Our three-fold pattern of worship is

- Welcome
- Equip
- Send

Welcome serves as the entrance rite as God's people gather and prepare to experience what God has prepared for us. *Equip* extends God's Word into song, sermon, and sacrament. *Send* focuses the worshippers on the challenge from God's Word and sends them into the world to serve in Jesus' name.

A Few Do's and Don'ts

As you move through this book, you'll go from the philosophical to the more specific. So stick with me here! By the time you reach the final chapter, you'll be ready to put it all together. That's when I'll give you an actual example of a mission-driven worship service that you can adapt and try out in your own church. But for now, here are a few general tips that can keep you heading in the right direction.

- **DO** *make the whole worship experience the message, not just the sermon.* The experience of worship begins in the parking lot and extends to the restrooms, to the chairs, to the service, to the coffee. So, are your parking lot and signage inviting? Do your restrooms make worshippers comfortable? Can people find a place to engage in the event? The whole experience needs to be *gospel*. It all needs to breathe gospel. It all *is* gospel because it is the message. Is everything about the experience welcoming, inclusive, focused, challenging, worthwhile, and transformational?

- **DO** *learn to celebrate mystery and communicate clearly—simultaneously!* Worship should provide a forum for clear communication of objective truth while, at the same time, celebrate all that is not understandable about God. We should be concerned about what people will take home with them. What new insight, spiritual truth, or life application will they grasp? And we should avoid trying to explain everything about God.

Worship, after all, is about a meeting of the mundane with the transcendent. We hope to come into the presence of what is much higher and greater than ourselves, the infinite. Obviously, we can't explain it all, and the gospel itself has always been proclaimed as a profound, saving *mystery*. Thus in our worship, we learn, we fellowship, we hear the crystal-clear call of God. But we also fall back into the arms of the mysterious One who put this all together—the One we will never completely comprehend. Clarity and mystery make a wonderful combination for worship!

• **DON'T** *neglect "outside-in" thinking.* Worship is a reflection of a congregation's building blocks. Any new worship initiative must reflect a commitment by a church's leadership to "outside-in" thinking. Instead of beginning with "what our congregation prefers," we must seriously consider the needs of those outside the church and how we can address those needs and perceptions within the worship environment. This evangelistic perspective presumes that the leadership is comfortable serving a larger community than its own.

The most effective outreach is for church members to invite their friends. If your people are confident about the quality and consistency of the worship experience, they will be motivated to invite others to attend. This is the wide-open front door of the church. People might say to their neighbors, "I'd like you to come to church with us because I know you'd love it." They are genuinely enthusiastic about the worship event, and that makes them genuinely effective evangelists.

And no one has to tell them to get excited about church; they're already enthused! The word *enthused* comes from the Greek *en-theos*, that is, "in God." People who are "in God" can become incredibly enthused. What drives that enthusiasm? A worship service that is compelling, meaningful, and worthwhile.

We need to understand and remember that people have many more choices on Sunday morning than they did twenty years ago, and the church is further down the list for most people. But relationships are important. The invitation of a friend to a compelling, meaningful worship service has all the ingredients for a win-win situation. Effective worship is directly related to effective evangelism.

• **DON'T** *confuse renewing worship with "youth programming."* New worship is much more than just a new way to get teens into church. In fact, it isn't age-related programming in any sense, although some approach it that way. Some might say, "If we get a new, hip worship thing started, then we'll get the kids back." But worship shouldn't be treated merely as a youth program, and every Sunday can't feel like "youth Sunday."

Research just doesn't substantiate an association between age and appreciation for contemporary worship. If the goal is to bring youth back into the church, the strategy should be to develop effective youth programming. Once in church worship, teens might find a new worship form more relevant, but people-programs are still the key to involving them in the life of the church.

At our church, we have a high school choir of over three hundred meeting on Wednesday nights. Over half of their two-hour rehearsal time is spent in Bible study, prayer, and discussion. Some of their time (thirty-five minutes) is devoted to learning music for worship and for their spring tour. Twenty minutes of their time together is devoted to worship—learning how to praise and listen to God together.

Many of these teens worship at our church services during the weekend as well, and some of them worship at other churches. But if they didn't have that formative Wednesday night, I doubt they would choose to worship at all. Here is a real-life example of genuine community based on a "cell" that creates a vibrant music ministry and a worshipping congregation of teenagers. Would they be there just for a choir practice? No. Only 7 percent would come for the music alone. Rather, they come for what they cannot get in school—authentic Christian relationships in a safe environment where they can ask their most pressing questions.

Experience the Joy!

The bottom line is that worship needs to incorporate objective truth with our subjective faith experience. Worship needs to be a reflection of real faith experience. All of Scripture is a testimony to real faith and life experience with God. Most churches choose, instead, to offer an objective experience of God—we sing and hear about the One we worship, but we rarely hear how it translates into the lives of real people, day by day.

Things get bogged down.

It all becomes a drag.

But there's a better way.

One of the joys of new, mission-driven worship forms is the possibility of real people sharing their first-hand experiences with God in an unscripted encounter within the congregation. That's when we have the opportunity to not only rejoice in the objective reality of the Creator of the universe, but engage in a dialogue about how this God "translates" into our everyday lives.

On one level, what we're talking about here is quite simple. Amidst our informed philosophy, effective scheduling, and practical structuring, we can

- share with one another God's answers to our prayers;
- tell stories of God's goodness in our daily lives;
- marvel at new miracles amidst our modern struggles;
- touch a brother or sister with our ideas, our hearts, our warm embraces;
- reflect on God's presence in the midst of intense pain;
- weep together;
- rejoice in the wonder;
- lift up our hearts and hands to God; or...

How would you do it in your church?

CHECKPOINTS

1. How would you describe your "philosophy of worship"? What aspects of worship in this chapter made the most impact on you? Why?

2. List some of the strengths of your church's current worship practices. What are some weaknesses?

3. Take a moment to brainstorm possible solutions to your worship weaknesses. Which ideas have some real possibilities? What first steps toward change could you begin immediately? What solutions will take some long-term planning with the entire congregation?

4. Which of the do's and don'ts made the most sense to you? Why? Did you disagree with anything there? Explain.

SUMMARY POINTS

1. Worship is what gives theological structure to the rest of the church organism.

2. Worship is about what God is doing.

3. Worship is God-focused and people-active.

4. Worship is scheduled every week at a regular time, and this schedule places worship in "prime time" during midmorning.

5. Options added to the worship schedule do not replace existing ones, but rather add times and diversity to a worshipper's choices.

6. The structure of worship should build upon the four-fold pattern and creatively include new elements and artistic ideas.

7. The whole worship experience is the message, not just the sermon.

8. Worship can simultaneously celebrate mystery and communicate clearly.

9. Worship begins with "outside-in" thinking.

10. Worship reflects objective truth and subjective faith experience.

Notes: Chapter 2

1. Barna Research Online, "Worship Tops the List of Important Church-Based Experiences" (February 19, 2001), www.barna.org.

2. Barna, "Worship Tops the List..." (February 19, 2001), www.barna.org.

CHAPTER 3

OK, So What Will the Future Church Be Like?

"But we never did it that way before!"

"You know what? You'll never do it that way again, either."

No, I can't imagine a pastor or other leader responding that way to a distressed church member. However, for most churches, it is a pretty *accurate* response. You see, the future church is emerging. And soon things just aren't going to be the same.

Ever again.

What will this emerging church look like? How will it be faithful to the gospel message in a millennium transitioning at light speed? Or will the church even be viable in the year 2050? Many church futurists are telling us that if we want to know what the emerging church will be like, we need to look closely at the first church. In other words, the church of the coming century may look a lot like the church of the first century.

But what exactly does that mean? In this chapter we'll take a little journey through several "lists," or at-a-glance descriptors, that show what the emerging church is probably going to be like. We'll do it under three main headings: sets of contrasting polarities, statements of reordered priorities, and trends in cultural and counter-cultural influences.

So...are you ready for the church of the future...*your* church?

It Will Avoid Deadly Polarities

The future church won't be so "black and white" in its approach to ministry. That may seem a bit scary at first, but we're not talking about compromising eternal, objective truths. Rather, the church will do better at holding in tension its *resonating* and *countering* ministries. Failing to do so throws a church into unproductive polarities that can kill the life of the Spirit within it. You'll see what I mean in just a moment, but let me stress here that *pursuing polarities will always lead the church to a place it shouldn't be.* In the coming decades, churches will recognize that either-or propositions are counterproductive. Polarities chill the soul and wound the well-intended. Consider:

Names vs. Numbers. I know there are negative feelings about the church-growth movement, and I can understand that negativity if success is equated with numbers alone. Numbers do not measure success in the context of worship. Whether your congregation totals seventy-five or seventy-five hundred makes little difference. Success comes when one person experiences the transformational love of Jesus Christ in worship. It can happen in Milton, North Dakota; in Burnsville, Minnesota; and wherever the people of God gather in Jesus' name. We can *simultaneously* celebrate a growing, expanding, culture-influencing church that involves more and more people for a greater and higher purpose than a good-looking annual report.

Same vs. Different. We have grown through an era where great effort was expended to start and maintain churches that all looked quite similar in their ministry efforts. In the future church, distinctiveness will be valued and diversity will be celebrated. What you do in your setting may be quite different from what we do at Prince of Peace, and that is exactly the way it should be. In your local setting, it's a blessing for your church to look and feel much different from the church down the street. One joy of the future church will be the contextualized expressions that exist alongside that which is globally common. Our differences and similarities can be appreciated and blessed. We are much the same—yet, at the same time, very different.

Traditional vs. Contemporary. At Prince of Peace we invest a great deal of time, money, and attention in the planning and leading of all kinds of worship experiences each week. But we have stopped using the divisive language of "traditional" or "contemporary." We simply name a service by describing it and allow people to make their own decisions regarding how and when they choose to worship. When surveyed, our congregation clearly preferred a more "contemporary" service, but over half of all our worshippers attend a service based primarily on the time of day that it's offered. Attempts to label worship styles seem to be a slippery slope leading to some kind of inaccurate descriptions. Simply stated, we focus on the *substance* of the worship events rather than the style. We currently offer six different kinds of worship substance during a weekend, and rarely does someone ask if a service is traditional or contemporary.

The question is not whether we sing traditional hymns or contemporary songs in a worship service. Rather, the key question has to do with how those songs are sung. What is the substance of the experience? What is the text saying to us today? And how are people welcomed into the event? A traditional service can be as welcoming to a first-time visitor as a contemporary one. So, in some ways, all of our services are exactly the same. In other ways, they are remarkably different.

Seekers vs. Believers. Much has been written lately regarding "seeker" services and their role within the evangelistic plan of a church. But in our experience, we find a lot of the "believer" in our seekers! Categorizing people rarely accomplishes much good.

We think that a seeker would want to experience what Christians do when they get together rather than a watered-down version that supposedly won't offend them. We believe it's possible for all worship to be "seeker sensitive"; that is, we always acknowledge the presence of first-time, unannounced worshippers. We can worship in our more "traditional" hour in such a way that it will be welcoming to all. In other words, we should assume the presence of both seekers and believers in our services and behave accordingly.

Everyone vs. Demographic Slices. Some would contend that, in order for worship to be effective, we must target particular worship events to particular demographic groups in the community. While this would be expedient and probably effective, it's not an accurate picture of what the church can be. Weekend worship ought to presume that anyone of any age or life experience can come and experience the presence of God in some way. Maybe not everything that occurs will speak to all, but somewhere there's a point of connection, regardless of age or life situation.

Worship is for everyone, not just Gen-Xers or Baby Boomers. Yet we can provide clearly focused worship possibilities for specific demographic populations within a community. High school kids should worship together as well as worship with their families and friends. A second grader should worship with church school classes in an age-appropriate expression and also worship with his or her family. Once again, it's "both and," not "either-or."

It Will Totally Retool Its Priorities

The future church will have vastly differing priorities from ours mainly because it will clearly recognize that we don't worship in a vacuum. We exist in a context, an environment, a neighborhood, a society. Therefore, what we are doing has broad implications that extend far beyond the church building.

I've already said that worship both *resonates with* the culture and *goes counter to* the culture around us. In resonating, the gospel doesn't exist in a bubble held separate from the experience of day-to-day living. We need to be aware of our community and the individual needs it represents. We need to have a sense of family schedules and pressures. We need to know when soccer games occur on the weekends. We need to know when parent-teacher conferences are scheduled. We need to know when the band trips are planned. We're not just talking about demographic issues, but sociological preferences, such as knowing which kinds of music people tune in on the radio, which CDs they buy, and which restaurants they prefer. Worship planners need to be mindful of the community in which they live. *And all of this will drastically affect the priorities of the future church!*

We'll talk more about counter-cultural influences in the next section of this chapter, but first let's get specific about the resonating ministry of worship and how it ought to affect a church's priorities. The following is a rather long list (but helpful, I hope!) of priority shifts that you can study now and perhaps come back to later. It could make a good topic list for an extended discussion in your cell groups or ministry teams. However you use it, it offers a pretty good idea of how your church will need to revamp its priorities in the years ahead.

From Membership to Discipleship. The future church will no longer invite people into membership in a church; it will invite them to consider the call of the Holy Spirit and become disciples of Jesus. We are not just another club to join. No, the church is the transformational body of Christ doing the work of creating a new and different world.

From Organization to Organism. The future church will pay close attention to the organic nature of the relationships that make the body work. Less time will be focused on organizational structures and more time will be spent in nurturing the relationships among people and helping them find their gifts and callings.

From Committee to Team. The future church will allow passionate Christians to engage in direct ministry related to their spiritual gifts. Ministry teams will "do" ministry without having to spend hours in deciding the specifics of how, when, and where the ministry will be done. Ministry will be accomplished by ministry teams.

From Money to Time. The future church will recognize that time is the new critical currency of the emerging culture. This church will recognize that people are *not* always asking, "How much will this cost?" They are asking, "How much time will it take?" The future church will value people's time.

From Doing to Equipping. The church of the future will equip the "priesthood of all believers" to do the ministry of the church rather than hiring more professionals to do it. These sinner-saints will be equipped to live out their faith in the real world, apart from the prompting of a church leader.

From Modern to Postmodern. The church will recognize that we are living in a new era, one that has never been lived through before and is radically different from any previous era. This church will recognize that our youth will not grow up and become just like us, even in the way they think and witness. It will see that the brains of those raised in this era are "wired" differently and that this fact presents the church with an opportunity to learn new ways to share the gospel story.

From Knowledge to Experience. The future church will finally recognize that the concept of objective truth just isn't recognized anymore in a postmodern world. This church will seek to provide opportunities for all to experience the love of God and share that love with others in tangible ways. Personal faith experience and story will be a new source of knowledge.

From Rational to Paradoxical. This church recognizes that almost all of life in this millennium is more paradoxical than rational. One plus one does not always equal two, and ministry needs to occur in a world where life is more gray than black and white.

From Participation to Involvement. The church of the future will seek deep and transformational involvement from individuals, not just participation. Numbers of people participating will not be the measure of success; transformed lives will be the measure.

From Felt Needs to Vertical Focus. Future churches will not focus their energies on perceived needs. They will initiate ministries with a vertical focus that changes the look of the horizon for everyone.

From Scripted Interaction to Spontaneous Interaction. Recognizing the power of story, the church of the future will, in the worship environment, move from scripted interaction among people to more spontaneous interaction. The church will recognize the importance of genuine, heartfelt, honest interchange within the worship space.

From Religious to Spiritual. The church of the future will tap into the incredible spiritual hunger of the emerging generations to seek new avenues for spiritual experience and development. People would rather be "spiritual" rather than "religious."

From Hospitality to Invitation. The future church will realize that simply being "warm and welcoming" is not enough to grow a church into the new millennium. The personal, compelling invitation to another person to "come and experience" is the way the church will grow.

From "Old or New" to "Old and New." The church of the future will recognize the power in fusing the old and new together to form something quite unique and compelling. If the worship world of a church operates with an either-or mentality, it will short-circuit the possibilities that exist.

From Music to Art. The future church will regard all forms of art as potentially useable within the context of worship. These churches will see music as just one of many ways to bless worshippers.

From Print to Visual. The church will begin to see an unlimited vista in the world of visual art to stimulate imaginations, inspire thinking, and enhance worship. Film, photography, painting, sculpture, and all forms of visual art will find their rightful place in the world of worship.

From Local to Global. The world is getting smaller. The Internet has created a superhighway for the instant sharing of ideas, information, and commerce. Our concerns are everyone's concern. Our world is not just our world, but everybody's world.

From Low Expectation to High Expectation. The future church will be a high-expectation organism whose life and purpose is to transform the globe into a new and different place. Persons of all kinds will want to affiliate with this church because of its great power and infinite possibilities for change. Discipleship will be its outcome, not membership.

From Change Me to Change the World. This church will know that the narcissistic implosion of the '90s is over and was always empty. The new frontier is the challenge and opportunity to make a difference for *everyone.*

From Linear to Concentric. The worship environment of the future church will engage all the senses in an overlapped and concentric experience where worshippers are doing many things at one time. Something may start and continue while a new element is added. Visuals, text, and music will be woven together in a tapestry of depth and tactile experience.

From a "Talking Head" to Communication. This church will seek to clearly communicate the texts and messages for the day in new and creative ways that integrate spoken word, text, visuals, examples, story, witness, and experience. This church will know that not everyone responds favorably to thirty minutes of a talking head.

From Denominations to Networks. Churches of the future will seek out alliances with other churches that have complementary missions and an affinity for each other's work. These alliances won't necessarily be based on denominational loyalty, but will spring from common affinities, purposes, and passions.

From Truth to Story. The church of the future will learn how to proclaim the truth of Jesus Christ boldly without seeming to be condemning or self-righteous in the process. The church will reclaim the power of story and tell it in new and significant ways.

From "Come and See" to Multisensory. Future churches will explore all the senses within the context of worship. The full experience of the goodness of God will include touch, taste, and smell, as well as seeing and hearing. These sensory experiences will overlay one another so that the sum of the event is far greater than any one of its parts.

From Knowledge to Mystery. The future church will embrace the mystery of God in new ways and begin to "know" God in fluid, focused, intentional times of worship. It will be OK to leave questions unanswered and all the possibilities open.

From Local Church to Mission Outpost. The church of the future will see itself as a mission outpost in the middle of a territory that isn't necessarily friendly to the message and ministry it has to share. It will assume the presence of those who need to hear, and operate as if their very existence depended on it.

From Rural/Suburban to Urban. This church will be quick to recognize that the social problems of the inner city are present and active, regardless of one's address. It will discard the notion that the "burbs" are safe and that rural America lives far from the issues of the city. It will decide to minister with "eyes wide open."

From Bad Coffee to Great Coffee. The church of the future will identify the trend of a society that values a great cup of coffee. It will desire to be a place where anyone who comes through the door can enjoy the company of passionate Christians and sip on excellently prepared Java. No kidding! The emerging church will value excellence and won't settle for mediocrity in anything.

It Will Maintain Its "Countering" Influence

Having said all of this about resonating with the culture, we still need to remember that part of the church's calling is to be a *counter*-cultural influence in the world. After all, we do need to stand against many things: the over-busyness of life; the disintegration of the family; the coarsening of the culture; and all the violent, materialistic trends that seem to get worse and worse. We need to rail against a self-centered culture that makes each of us the center of our own universe. And worship can be the safe haven away from the trappings of such a culture. Worship can be that quiet place in the middle of the noise.

If we were to examine several of the trends in the culture with a "countering eye," what would it mean for the church? Let's try it! Below, you'll see several trend-categories (which echo most of the priority shifts in the section above) with a cultural statement and an accompanying countering concept that the church of the future will need to offer in response. In effect, these responses demonstrate the counter-cultural opportunities that will come to the church in the future—opportunities to be "salt and light," to be *in* the world but not *of* the world (see 1 John 2:15-17).

DISCIPLESHIP

CULTURE SAYS: "I suppose I could be a member as long as it doesn't cost me anything."

COUNTER: Discipleship is high-cost and high-expectation. Your church's numerical growth may screech to a halt.

In mission-driven worship, everything focuses on making disciples.

ORGANISM

CULTURE SAYS: "If we just get *organized*, we'll be able to decide what to do and assign someone to do it."

COUNTER: When the church lives as an organism, it forces leaders into real relationships in order to accomplish ministry. This is not doing by delegation.

In worship, pay attention to "chance" meetings in the hallways.

TEAM

CULTURE SAYS: "Form a committee, run it by Robert's Rules of Order, and the most votes will have the power."

COUNTER: Teamwork is culturally understood, but radical for a church. The real power is at the point of ministry, not at the committee meeting.

In worship, ministry teams accomplish everything that is necessary.

TIME

CULTURE SAYS: "If I can just make enough money, everything will be all right."

COUNTER: In a world that values accumulation and things, the church needs to place priority value on how time is spent.

In worship, value everyone's time more than their money; spend both of them wisely.

EQUIPPING

CULTURE SAYS: "In my business, if I want something done, I hire someone to do it."

COUNTER: In the church, we all—not just the pastor—do real ministry.

In worship, model the priesthood of all believers, with lay ministers involved in every aspect of worship.

EXPERIENCE

CULTURE SAYS: "My greatest experience of the week was watching the latest Hollywood film."

COUNTER: In a culture that loves to watch others engage in life (through film and TV), the counter-cultural message is "You can do more than just watch; come and experience."

In worship, work hard to make it a come-and-engage experience.

INVOLVEMENT

CULTURE SAYS: "The only thing churches are interested in is adding another number to their rolls."

COUNTER: Let's measure success by the personal transformation of each life.

In worship, offer opportunities for individual encounters by anointing with oil, kneeling for prayer, and encouraging pairing up for personal prayers.

VERTICAL FOCUS

CULTURE SAYS: "I'm the center of my universe."

COUNTER: Guess what? The church says you're *not* the center of your universe. Now that's radical!

In worship, point to the radical counter-cultural message of other-centeredness.

SPONTANEOUS INTERACTION

CULTURE SAYS: "The church would be the last place to find people who are honest about their doubts and failures."

COUNTER: The road to spiritual illumination is through self-disclosure.

In worship, be honest and open about real stuff. God can take it.

SPIRITUAL EXPERIENCE

CULTURE SAYS: "If I have enough 'toys,' I won't have to think about spiritual issues."

COUNTER: All the stuff of life can't fill the empty place in a person's soul.

In worship, always point to God as the giver of all things and the one who can fill that empty place in the human soul.

INVITATION

CULTURE SAYS: "My faith is a private and personal reality. I will not impose it on anyone."

COUNTER: We may need to step out of our comfort zone and not only invite someone to come, but go and pick them up. (Our culture would tell us that an adequate ad campaign is sufficient, or worse, that inviting just doesn't matter.)

In worship, celebrate a public Christianity.

OLD AND NEW

CULTURE SAYS: "New is good. Retro is great. Old is bad."

COUNTER: We know better. We hold in our hearts the Author of all that is old, all that is current, and all that will be.

In worship, sing and experience the old along with the new.

ART

CULTURE SAYS: "Art and music? The church is the last place I'd go to experience either."

COUNTER: Creativity and innovation are gifts from God that we can celebrate in worship. Art is a conduit for the transcendent.

In worship, reach for excellence, stimulate creativity, and bless innovation.

VISUAL

CULTURE SAYS: "I get my visual stimulation from MTV. That's all I need."

COUNTER: We need to use art to stimulate imagination. The imagination is far greater than artificially projected images.

In worship, use images to stimulate, not to substitute. Encourage worshippers to close their eyes and run their own videotapes in their mind's eye.

POSTMODERN

CULTURE SAYS: "Those kids will grow up to be just like us. This is just a phase they're going through. We went through it, and we turned out all right."

COUNTER: The emerging generations are not just a new e-commerce target. They're several generations that think, believe, and act in new and different ways. The counter-cultural challenge is to chip through the veneer to find out what's really inside.

In worship, reflect the need of postmoderns in every way possible. Study their culture and create unique ways to communicate.

PARADOXICAL

CULTURE SAYS: "We'd like to believe there's a right and wrong to every difficult issue."

COUNTER: It's not so. It's not necessary. As Christians, we will learn how to live in a world of paradox.

In worship, greet paradox with glee. Celebrate the complexities of life while pointing to Scripture as source and Holy Spirit as guide.

GLOBAL

CULTURE SAYS: "We're the greatest nation on earth, and I want my piece of the pie."

COUNTER: We don't have the luxury of behaving as if we're the only people on the planet while continuing to consume most of its resources.

In worship, always pray for the global church and the concerns of the whole world.

HIGH EXPECTATION

CULTURE SAYS: "I don't want anything to do with an organization that doesn't know what it wants from me."

COUNTER: The church needs to emerge from its marginalized corner of society, where faith is secretive and ministry has no hope of countering the wave of secular culture.

In worship, remind everyone that the call to discipleship will lead us on a pathway similar to the one that Christ walked. This is not a path of untainted glory; it is a path of suffering and service.

CHANGE THE WORLD

CULTURE SAYS: "I have this feeling that the world might be bigger than me and my needs."

COUNTER: Hello…you aren't the center of the universe.

In worship, remind everyone of the global calling of Christ—to make a new and different world in God's name.

CONCENTRIC

CULTURE SAYS: "If we can keep God limited to the linear, logical, and rational, we can simply avoid the possibility of a multilayered tactile experience of God."

COUNTER: We need to begin to see God at work in simultaneously overlapping and logarithmically charged experiences.

In worship, do more than one thing at once.

COMMUNICATION

CULTURE SAYS: "Preachers? You'd need to have the speaking skills of Tom Brokaw to compete for my attention."

COUNTER: The cultural expectation is that the church can't communicate effectively. But we can be open to learning how to use multiple mediums to communicate.

In worship, use every tool at your disposal to communicate effectively.

NETWORKS

CULTURE SAYS: "Churches are just competing with one another."

COUNTER: Churches working together, building on each other's strengths and weaknesses for the common good, would shatter this cultural expectation.

In worship, pray for neighboring churches and the common mission you share. Remind worshippers of joint ventures and the power of united ministries.

STORY

CULTURE SAYS: "Christians are all self-righteous hypocrites, aren't they?"

COUNTER: We can discover new ways to be passionate and motivated Christians, destroying the cultural expectations about us.

In worship, tell the stories, don't preach the dogma. Let the text do the talking.

MULTISENSORY

CULTURE SAYS: "Christians just sit and listen to a preacher talk about his or her version of the truth.

COUNTER: Good worship will explode these preconceptions.

In worship, let worshippers experience God through all the senses.

MYSTERY

CULTURE SAYS: "The church thinks it has a corner on the truth. It places a high value on knowing the truth and being sure of salvation, right?"

COUNTER: When the church embraces mystery, we widen the circle of invitation and demonstrate our honesty and openness to the things of God.

In worship, celebrate mystery. Be open about what's impossible to know.

MISSION OUTPOST

CULTURE SAYS: "Thank God that little church on the corner doesn't bother us."

COUNTER: The church is the only organism that exists for the benefit of those who haven't been there yet.

In worship, share local concern and ministry projects. Gather support for outreaching to the community.

URBAN

CULTURE SAYS: "People in the church don't have any idea what we're going through in our family."

COUNTER: We need to learn what families are going through and decide how we can help.

In worship, challenge people to actively participate in making their communities the best places they can be.

GREAT COFFEE

CULTURE SAYS: "Church? That's the last place I'd go to have a cup of coffee."

COUNTER: Why can't the church be the first and best place one would think of to not only have a great cup of coffee but also find a warm, welcoming environment to engage in significant conversations regarding the issues of life and death?

In worship (or next door to worship), provide a great cup of coffee and a warm, welcoming environment. The rest may happen on its own.

How did you like your glimpse of the emerging church and what worship might look and feel like in the future? The thing that is so intriguing is that we can look at this future church and see, for the most part, an accurate picture of the ancient church described in Acts 2. And that's good news!

"They devoted themselves to the apostles' teaching and fellowship, to the breaking of bread and the prayers. Awe came upon everyone,

because many wonders and signs were being done by the apostles. All who believed were together and had all things in common; they would sell their possessions and goods and distribute the proceeds to all, as any had need. Day by day, as they spent much time together in the temple, they broke bread at home and ate their food with glad and generous hearts, praising God and having the goodwill of all the people. And day by day the Lord added to their number those who were being saved" (ACTS 2:42-47, NRSV).

CHECKPOINTS

1. In what ways does your church resonate with the culture these days? How does it seek to *counter* the culture? What improvements could be made in both of these ministries?

2. List the apparent priorities of your church's mission and worship. How do these compare and contrast to the list of priorities laid out in this chapter?

3. As you have read about the trends in the culture, which made the most impact on you? Why?

4. Which characteristics of the future church are most exciting and compelling for you? Which are most fearful? Why?

5. Name some first steps your church could take toward the future. What are the top three things that would have to happen first?

SUMMARY POINTS

1. The church of the next century might look like the church of the first century.

2. New movements do not imply the loss of what was, but a layering of what is to come.

3. As a first-world church, we are being impacted by postmodern realities of emerging generations.

4. Because emerging generations are wired differently, we are called to minister in new ways.

5. The new church will be able to simultaneously hold multiple realities in tension with one another and move forward with mission and ministry.

CHAPTER 4

Tap the Power of Worship Teams

Pastor: Do you say your prayers at night, little boy?

Jimmy: Yes, sir.

Pastor: And do you always say them in the morning, too?

Jimmy: No, sir. I ain't scared in the daytime.

This anonymous snippet of conversation lends more than just a little humor to our study. It's insightful, too, reminding us that everything we're talking about in the way of change must be bathed in prayer by all concerned—day and night.

And it is scary!

Transitions are always a bit fearful. But some of them bring the most amazing good things to us, blessings we never expected. I think it's that way with transitioning into the way of the future church, the mission-driven organism we've been exploring.

For example, one of the great transitions of recent years has been the movement from a Lone Ranger mentality to the power of team. This may be scary for some pastors. And it's certainly a daunting experience for congregations accustomed to letting a paid professional staff do all the work of the ministry. However, in the new era, pastors will not write sermons all alone on a Saturday night after thinking up a topic from their solitary musings. Organists won't just play what they want to play, based purely on their artistic preferences. Choir directors won't frantically pick their Sunday music on Wednesday night. And soloists won't just sing a song because it fits into their vocal range so nicely. Why? Because every aspect of worship will be planned together in team and accomplished through the power of team.

If that's going to be a scary thing for your church at the moment, please stick with me. This chapter can help dispel some of your misgivings. After all, two heads are better than one, and five heads are even better than that! Thinking, creating, and implementing are always better when accomplished by team effort.

I can't give you the perfect picture of how it will work in your own church, but we can hit a few highlights that may put you on the path to creative planning. Specifically, let's think about: What qualities you'll want in your worship team leaders; what types of teams you'll need for effective worship planning; and what it takes to do music right, from ensemble organization to music selection.

About Your Worship Team Leaders

Teams require leadership. And this new leadership might look re-markably different from the leadership of the past. In fact, worship in the future will require a new kind of leader. For example, this leader

- will be a direct conduit for the vision and mission of the organism.
- will be a coach, mentor, and nurturer of leadership relation-ships—not an executive decision maker.
- will lead by example, having the primary ability to build and lead a team at a variety of levels.
- will be able to identify, equip, and employ the passions and skills of people within the worship and music environment.
- will not primarily be a doer/player/singer/musician. This leader will be a planner/giver/helper/enabler.

The potential exists for a worship leader/musician to get out of the way and eventually stand at the back of the church and watch it all happen. The musician's goal shifts from worship leader to mentor in order to empower the people to fully lead the worship event. An ef-fective music director assumes a coaching role—gathering talent and nurturing enthusiasm within a congregation, organizing it into sys-tems that make sense, and deploying it in a compelling manner. In this way we are effectively returning ministry to the priesthood of believers, who now can be team members.

*"As you come to him, the living Stone—rejected by men but cho-
sen by God and precious to him—you also, like living stones,
are being built into a spiritual house to be a holy priesthood, offering spiritual sacrifices acceptable to God through Jesus Christ.
For in Scripture it says: "See, I lay a stone in Zion, a chosen
and precious cornerstone, and the one who trusts in him will
never be put to shame."*

*"...you are a chosen people, a royal priesthood, a holy nation, a
people belonging to God, that you may declare the praises of
him who called you out of darkness into his wonderful light"*
(1 PETER 2:4-6, 9).

Not just the professionals—but all of us—are called to bring praise
and glory to God in worship. In other words, team members are not
necessarily church staff members. They are not necessarily paid. But
they are team members because their skills and passions relate to
the discussion on the table. And they gather at the invitation of the
leader in any place, at anytime.

About the "Big Three " Team Types

Throughout the ministry of the church,
numerous new teams might be created that function for specific
tasks, moving from the most
global of concerns to the most
specific implementations.
When it comes to worship,
in particular, we like to organize things around the Big
Three: the Thematic Team,
the Creative Team, and the
Service-Leading Team(s). Let's
look briefly at each of them.

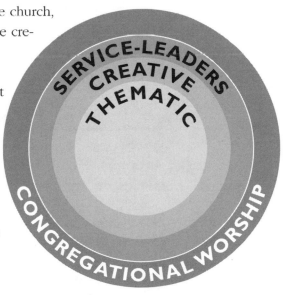

THEMATIC TEAM

This group works on the development of worship texts and themes several months or years in advance. If your church uses a lectionary, it would be a key tool for this group. Team members would "translate" the Scripture texts into worship themes; sermon topics; and creative music, art, and drama ideas. Team members would likely include:

- the pastor, who brings assigned texts to the table. The pastor also represents the congregational concerns regarding vision and mission.
- a teacher, who can represent the developmental needs of children and their families and interpret proposed themes on their behalf.
- a musician, who can envision the creative use of music to enhance selected text and themes.
- an artist, who can translate text into metaphor, metaphor into visual art, and then speak on behalf of a group of nontextual learners.
- a teen minister, who can visualize how the text and theme will impact teen populations and their families.

The Scripture texts or lessons determine the direction for the thematic structure of worship and all elements of the music-art-drama. It is further possible to have these texts and themes saturate all of church life for the entire week in adult studies, teen programming, children's worship, and all other worship. I'm sure you can imagine how it might be done in your congregation.

Yes, this thematic approach takes more effort, ongoing advanced planning, and an attitude of intense cooperation. But the results will be well worth the extra attention. This approach to programming begins with—and returns to—the centrality of worship. The primary tasks of this team would be

- to look at the assigned texts for the given days of the year;
- to determine what critical messages and themes will be shared with the congregation through these texts;

- to select three important things to focus on in worship as outgrowths of these texts and theme; and
- to distribute these proposed texts and themes for reflection and reaction from others in the staff and the entire congregation.

CREATIVE TEAM

This team works at least two months in advance to prepare and plan the specifics of each worship event, including songs, hymns, sketches, visuals, arts, and drama. The worship leader who knows and appreciates the power of team will assemble those who can contribute to a process much bigger than any of them. The Creative Team might meet for one hour each week around the text and theme for worship events in the near future. Members of this team can be paid or unpaid staff. They might include:

- a pastor, who brings the text to life with theological perspective.
- a children's leader, who translates the needs of kids, teens, and families in regard to worship.
- Web surfers, who can find the images and ideas to visualize the concepts.
- artists, who can move us through color and form.
- poets, who can use language to shape new horizons.
- musicians, who can lead singing and praising and do musical things that the assembly cannot.
- a lighting designer, who can focus our attentions on the proper places in the worship space.
- a photographer, who can see beyond "what is" to "what could be."
- a videographer, whose moving pictures tell our story.
- a technologist, who can integrate all the elements in the worship space.

The key operating principle: Everything to do with text, theme, and worship planning is a work in progress.

SERVICE-LEADING TEAM(S)

This team puts the specifics of the week together for each week—into print and projection form, as needed—and arranges for all the specific details of the week to be accomplished. It includes the leaders of each vocal-instrumental ensemble. Here's a brief description of each member's work.

• *Director of Worship and Music.* This leader directs, plans, and organizes the world of worship for the local church. He or she calls the appropriate service-leading teams together to work on specific tasks related to worship and music. The information from the Thematic Team and the Creative Team is put into play for the coming week's worship.

One of the key roles of the director of worship and music is to invite new team members into the process of leading worship. The process should include interviews and assessments of the skills and passions of persons being considered. If there seems to be a match, the invitation is extended to join one of the teams. The interview is critical to matching skill and passion with the musical needs of the congregation.

• *Organist.* The organist selects thematically appropriate hymns and picks worship music to enhance each event, based on the work of the Thematic Team. The organist may be asked to play in conjunction with "fused" worship elements (all forces working together) during the course of the worship services.

• *Choir directors and accompanists.* Because texts and themes were selected far in advance, choir directors have ordered and rehearsed music for the week that ties directly to the text and theme of the weekend worship. The choir sees itself as primary worship leader, leading all aspects of music in the service. The placement of the anthem maximizes the choir's impact in the service.

• *Instrumental ensemble directors.* They are aware of the thematic and seasonal thrust of the week and pick music to enhance the service. Instrumental ensembles will also be asked to fuse with other worship elements and accompany many musical selections, not just play a song.

• **Hospitality Leader.** Hospitality teams understand the dynamics of the coming week, and teams are put in place by the leaders of each area. Parking lot attendants, greeters, ushers, food hosts, information hosts, baptism hosts, and Communion servers are deployed, as needed.

• **Technology Leader.** The technology leader schedules the technicians for the week and prepares the various technological elements of the service. Occasionally the team may help to create a brief video that highlights a ministry or congregational need. The technical requirements of the worship team are considered, along with other art elements, to be sure all lighting, sound, and visual components will work together to tell the story in a compelling way.

• **Print Leader.** Printed materials are developed to serve the weekend worship. A folded 11x17 bulletin is prepared for every worshipper who will attend one of the many worship offerings. A Tool Kit (one per family), containing the prayer concerns of the church, the weekly devotional, and the other programming invitations (along with other Christian-growth materials) is printed.

Children's bulletins are printed, as well as brochures for special events and a newcomer's guide with information on the church. Leader's guides for each person leading worship are printed as well. These contain every event, movement, and technical detail for each service.

• **Worship Team Leaders.** Music packets and tapes are prepared so that musicians can pick them up ten days in advance of the worship they will lead. Team leaders rehearse with each of the bands for the week in a one-hour session.

About All Those Music Folks

"When David was old and full of days, he made his son Solomon king over Israel. David assembled all the leaders of Israel and the priests and the Levites. The Levites, thirty years

old and upward, were counted, and the total was thirty-eight thousand. 'Twenty-four thousand of these,' David said, 'shall have charge of the work in the house of the Lord, six thousand shall be officers and judges, four thousand gatekeepers, and four thousand shall offer praises to the Lord with the instruments that I have made for praise' " (1 CHRONICLES 23:1-5, NRSV).

Did you catch that? Four thousand skilled musicians for temple worship and praise! That's a lot of musicians. Wouldn't you love to have heard the sound they made? It must have been a raucous, jubilant praise music of a kind we've never experienced.

You may not be able to assemble a team of four thousand. But as you begin bringing together your musical volunteers, you'll probably be asking yourself at least two basic questions: "What kinds of people are we looking for?" and "How will we organize them?"

• **What to look for in service-leading team members.** First, look for passion in those who want to be leading services by using their musical gifts. Any service-leading team member has the skill and desire to serve Christ's church through worship. The musicians who are passionate about their calling, willing to make it a priority, and will be there for the long haul are far more valuable than the musicians who are in it to perfect their musical performance skills. Identify and recruit people who are both capable and willing, not necessarily those who are great musically. Although ability is certainly important, it is more important to use a musician who is available, on-task, and passionate about participating. Insist on a high level of responsibility and hold everyone to it.

Second, look for people who know how to lead group singing. The primary task of the musicians is to lead congregational song. Most of the music of worship will be congregational in nature, and strong leadership is necessary if we're going to engage reluctant singers. The effective ensemble clearly invites the worshipper to sing and makes it evident as to when and what the worshipper should be singing.

In fact, the focus of the ensemble is on the best instrument for leading worship: the human voice. What we really want to hear in worship is the honest sound of humanity singing in community and
with feeling. (You might consider singing unaccompanied for a
change. Have the organist sit out on the second verse. The human
voice is critical to good worship, and we need to teach worshippers
that they are essential to the worship event by contributing their
voices.) We need sopranos, altos, and tenors who not only read music and sing well, but whose vocal sound is more "pop" in quality.
This might involve a group of three or as many as a dozen singers.
They need to be able to sing on pitch and control their vibratos.
Anything less than this beginning requirement can lead to vocal-
team disaster.

Third, look for people who have no problem fusing with others.
What do I mean? Throughout a worship morning, at times all musical
forces will be asked to fuse—combine, blend, mix, mingle, work together—with others in the worship. The ensemble members will
learn the hymns and sing them. The organ may play with the ensemble, and the choir lead selected pieces of music. The instrumental
ensembles may accompany the organ on selected hymns. The choir
may sing the parts of the ensemble choruses. This is the beginning
of fusion. This is a team effort, and there is no "I" in T-E-A-M!

• *How to organize your instrumental ensemble teams.* I can't give
you by-the-numbers instructions about your instrumental groups because all churches are different and have unique needs and varying
resources. However, I do want to stress that the core of an instrumental ensemble is the rhythm section. Bass, drums, and guitar form
the nucleus of the musical power of the group that leads worship.
These musicians' intuition is important, as well as is their ability to
play together. This does not happen overnight, but only through
many months and years of playing together.

This critical core, in some settings, is a paid group of individuals
that lends consistency and quality to every new worship event on
an ongoing basis. This core is also a comfortable team to fall back

on in case a number of volunteers decide they cannot contribute on a given weekend. The core is present each week. In most settings, the instrumental ensembles consist of some or all of the following:

- a bass guitar
- drums
- a lead guitar
- a piano
- second keyboard (for layered sounds)
- acoustic guitar
- percussion, such as a conga, a shaker, and a triangle
- flute, sax, horns, and strings
- three to nine singers (sopranos, altos, and tenors)

The addition of an acoustic guitar, a second keyboard layer, and percussion instruments helps fill out the sound of the group and makes it possible for the group to lead more diverse kinds of music.

Service-Leading Team Organization

In our church, we use a team system of colors: red, green, blue, and yellow. Selected individuals are assigned to lead worship on a volunteer basis once per month. This allows each musician to know his or her schedule long into the future and avoid scheduling conflicts. They meet according to the following schedule:

> First weekend of every month—Red Team
> Second weekend of every month—Green Team
> Third weekend of every month—Blue Team
> Fourth weekend of every month—Yellow Team
> Occasional fifth weekends—randomly assigned teams.

In each of the weekend ensembles, you might choose to use solo instruments to enhance the sound of the ensembles. An example of how this might work is as follows:

- Red Team: flute
- Green Team: violin
- Blue Team: soprano sax
- Yellow Team: horn section (two trumpets, one trombone)

Depending upon the musicians' improvisational skills, music will need to be purchased or arranged to accommodate these players.

Now, how is everything scheduled? Ten days in advance of the weekend, you can put together a music packet that provides all of the song material for the coming worship services. Singers and musicians pick up the packets (and tapes) before they're to lead worship, and practice the music in advance of the rehearsal. Included in the packet is a devotional based on the text and theme of the coming weekend, and each ensemble member is encouraged to use the devotional for private or group study during the coming week. Also included is a prayer challenge to guide the prayers of the members for one another and for the concerns of the coming weekend. The music packet usually contains four to six pieces of music.

As far as rehearsal times go, we do it this way: On Tuesday at 5 p.m., the Sunday service-leading ensemble comes to the worship center to rehearse for one hour. The first half-hour is spent in a split rehearsal. The instrumental band rehearses separately from the singers, who work on notes and phrasing. The second half-hour is spent putting together what was learned so far. The ensemble assembles again forty-five minutes prior to the first service and puts the final touches on all the music for that morning.

Communication with team members is crucial, but can often be handled by telephone alone. With a well-established color-coded system, there is very little need for weekly reminders. Phone calls will be necessary when replacing those who are unable to lead on a given weekend. Several times per year, letters are mailed to all participants to communicate goals and indicate changes.

Finally, the Worship Director mails an evaluation form to allow participants to offer feedback, suggestions and/or criticism. This also provides a face-saving opportunity for anyone to exit the program if he or she chooses. Once per year the teams themselves are evaluated and then re-formed for the coming season.

About Music Selection: Some Concluding Thoughts

> *"Sing psalms and hymns and spiritual songs among yourselves, singing and making melody to the Lord in your hearts, giving thanks to God the Father at all times and for everything in the name of our Lord Jesus Christ"* (EPHESIANS 5:19-20, NRSV).

The church and its worship teams need to seriously consider the criteria they will use to select music so that, as Martin Luther once said, the Word of God is "driven into the heart with sweet song." Why not run all of your music through the following quality filters?

QUESTION 1:

Is this song true?

Is the message of the song true to life? Is it theologically correct? Is it consistent with our congregation's vision and mission? Be conscious of the sensitivities of those you might be trying to reach. For example, you might want to choose songs that avoid male pronouns for God and the Holy Spirit. Also be sensitive to images that may be offensive to some in the congregation, such as military imagery, gender-hierarchical language, and racially insensitive ideas. Include as many people as possible in the music you pick!

QUESTION 2:

Is the imagery powerful, relevant, and linked to our worship theme?

Look closely at the images that come through in the text. Do they fit the culture around you? Agricultural imagery does not work well for suburban Minneapolis. (We don't "plow the fields and scatter" here—we simply try to stay out of traffic!) Images of home or relationships are stronger for our community.

As a rule of thumb, pick songs that have depth and tactile imagery and that bear repetition. Good worship music uses deep imagery and metaphor and weaves together multiple concepts in artful ways for maximum impact. So...will this song indeed have *impact*? If it's just a nice little tune that happens to tie into the text, that's not a good enough reason to use it. Will the music, by its good construction, move a worshipper in some new way?

Finally, the song selections need to help tell the thematic text and story of worship. Do the images and outcomes of the song connect directly to what we're trying to communicate in this particular time of worship?

QUESTION 3:

Is this song generally singable by Jane and Joe Church-member?

Obviously, in every congregation there are a few folks who will never be able to carry a tune. We're not talking about them; we're aiming for the average person who wants to sing and can do it if the music isn't too intricate.

The point is, worship songs should be easy to sing, quick to learn, and hard to forget. Perhaps the bottom-line question, as far as singability goes, is this: *"Does the song teach itself?"* Good writing will structure a song so that it actually teaches itself. A degree of predictability is a trademark of pop music writing. If the song consists of eight unrelated musical ideas, some in the congregation may become frustrated. We ought to be able to invite people to listen the first time through and then join in whenever they feel comfortable (which should happen quickly).

One more thing about singability: A very practical matter in song selection is the performed length of the song. Not only will a congregation eventually tune out an extraordinarily long song, but the usual time constraints of worship may prohibit its use. To an American pop-radio culture, any musical selection that lasts more than three minutes will begin to feel quite long.

And remember that there's a difference between hymns and songs. Hymns tend to have enough poetic freight that it takes a lifetime to unpack them! Songs tend to take single concepts and walk around them from different perspectives. Songs usually don't attempt to tell the whole story of salvation in five stanzas. There is room for both in worship, but they are not the same.

Along these lines, stay sensitive to the clash of old and new. Some of what we're experiencing in worship renewal is the rebirth of the old in new wrappings. Let me suggest the following "new" songs, which work great with a large worship team:

- "Beautiful Savior"
- "Softly and Tenderly"
- "My Jesus, I Love Thee"
- "Great Is Thy Faithfulness"

Old or new isn't the issue; the real questions to ask yourself when including any worship song or hymn are "Is it a good song? and Is it timeless in its goodness?"

QUESTION 4:
Is this song in keeping with our emphasis on variety?

Yes, you should be seeking variety! Avoid a steady diet of songs that begin with "I," for instance. Strive for a good cross-section of subjective and objective elements. Worship should be God-focused and people-related, not the other way around. When we gather to worship, one of the movements that we hope will take place is the movement from "I" to "we." Separate individuals may gather, but are sent as "we."

Also use song material from diverse sources. For example, on a given weekend you might (if the text and theme allow) use musical styles such as spirituals, rock, blues, and jazz all in one worship event. And diversity covers not only source but theme as well. It means worship music should sing *joy* as well as *lament, cross* as well as *glory, pleasure* as well as *pain.* If the music consists only of up-tempo praise songs, it's conveying the wrong message about God's character and what it means to live as a servant of Christ.

To summarize: Depending on the text or the type of worship, we need to have a variety of song styles from which to choose. Which songs are appropriate? Which songs suit which musicians? Some songs will serve particular parts of the worship with dramatically different dynamic ranges. Songs before prayer should be quiet and meditative. Opening songs can gather people together in a raucous celebration. Sending songs can send God's people out with power to serve in the name of Jesus. Variety is the spice of worship.

QUESTION 5:
Is our use of this song legal?

We're talking copyright law here. When in doubt, get permission. Whenever you reprint anything at all, any words or music that are not of your own composition require permission from someone. There are no exceptions, and ignorance is not an excuse. The same restrictions hold true when copying an audiotape or CD for any purpose or recording a session or service that includes materials protected by copyright. To better understand the seriousness of this issue, just think of the music as a piece of property and the photocopy or tape as stolen goods.

Protect yourself and the property of others by planning ahead and asking permission. For worship music, contact CCLI (Christian Copyright Licensing, Inc.) at 1-800-234-2446. For video and film licensing, call the Motion Picture Licensing Corporation at 1-800-462-8855. Most publishers offer their own licensing, and if you are using a high percentage of one publisher's material, simply call them and they will arrange a licensing agreement for you.

CHECKPOINTS

1. Do you use worship teams in planning and running your services? If so, how well are they functioning?
2. If you are not currently using worship teams, what is your reaction to the idea? How practical would these be for your church? Why?
3. What principles of good music selection does your church practice? Which still need to be put into play?
4. How would you characterize the quality of your congregational singing? Which ideas in this chapter might help you improve?

SUMMARY POINTS

1. The mission of the emerging church is accomplished by ministry teams.
2. A ministry team leader's primary skills are coaching, mentoring, nurturing, building, administrating, identifying, and equipping all believers for ministry.
3. The thematic team works a year in advance to pick text and themes and determine three important things to shape the focus

of worship for that weekend. This team could work one season at a time in one meeting.

4. The creative team works two months in advance to prepare and plan the specifics of each worship including songs, hymns, sketches, visuals, arts, and drama.

5. The worship and music team puts the specifics of the week together for that week into print and projection form and arranges for all the specific details of the week to be accomplished.

6. The text must be true and help connect people with the Scripture text.

7. Choose diverse musical styles, using culturally relevant old and new music, mixing joy and lament.

8. Avoid language that could be offensive.

9. Pick music that is easy to sing, quick to learn, and hard to forget.

10. Pick music that will have "high impact" when it is used in worship.

CHAPTER 5

Space: The Final Frontier

Have you ever felt the "awe"?

I mean have you ever walked into a church and a warm sense of relaxation washed over you? Or maybe it was a profound sensation of awe. Or perhaps a spark of excitement that you could attribute only to a renewed awareness of the Spirit within you. In each case you knew you were on holy ground within sacred space, something that called to the depths of your being.

You had entered the presence of the Lord...

On the other hand, you may have walked into a church sanctuary and suddenly encountered discord. Maybe it was just the arrangement of the altar furniture or the uncoordinated color scheme. Or, if worship was in progress, maybe the sights and sounds in general just didn't seem compelling—for reasons mysteriously unknown to you.

Maybe it was just you.

Or maybe it was more than that.

All of us can agree: We'd rather have our own church convey the former kind of experience rather than the latter. But how do we do it? How do we make a great space for worship that is inviting and that prepares worshippers for all God wants to do in their hearts?

Set Up for Heaps of Hospitality

Clearly, we can't engineer the "awe." If God is in a place and seeks to speak to our hearts, he will do it regardless of the architecture or sound system. However, I do believe God calls us to be responsible in helping to prepare hearts for an awareness of his presence, rather than doing things that might hinder the movement of his Spirit. So we need to think carefully about our worship space and what it conveys.

So we need to think carefully about our worship space and what it conveys. Unfortunately, many churches give the distinct impression that the church grounds, parking lot, and worship area are private spaces, and *only members who understand the rules are welcome.* Churches may not think they communicate such a troubling bias, but it becomes fairly clear by everything they practice. How sad!

Every square foot of church property is public space and should be invitational. We should expect the arrival of first-time, unannounced visitors every week. These will be guests who don't know the parking rules, the location of the bathrooms, the schedules, and the expectations. They can't read signs that are too small or nonexistent, and they don't know how to find the coffee and rolls. They haven't memorized the songs or the responses and aren't keen on being embarrassed by not knowing what to do. If a congregation doesn't expect visitors or make them feel welcome, they probably won't appear. God might be about to nudge someone into attending church, but churches need to be ready to welcome him or her. I just can't say it enough: We need to be ready.

Here's a way to start: In your ministry teams, think through all the points of contact a visitor would have from the moment he or she enters your parking lot. Then brainstorm ways that those contact points could become opportunities for showering heaps of hospitality. For example, I would suggest you abandon the term *usher* and adopt "minister of hospitality" instead. The umbrella of hospitality extends to parking lot attendants, greeters, ushers, food hosts, baptism hosts, and communion servers. The team leaders of each group are responsible for working together and communicating with each other, as well as creating opportunities for these ministers to know one another.

Signage and parking problems often need to be addressed. If you're short on parking space, why not use a shuttle bus to access a locally unused parking lot? Set your worship times to allow transition in the parking lots to be as painless as possible—so people can actually arrive on time for your services.

A final note of caution: Don't forget your special-needs folks. Provide large print bulletins for those who need them. Provide hearing assistance devices for those who need them. Provide an ASL interpreter for those who need one. Provide wheelchair parking places in the worship space for those who need them. If the church is to be welcoming, using these four suggestions will go a long way toward providing access to all who want to come, hear, see, and experience the love of God in worship.

Gear Up for Gathering

"Sense of gathering" is an architectural term that refers to the mood a space conveys when it makes people feel part of a gathered community. How do you create it? Well, just as an example, suppose you were to replace the traditional pew lineup of straight rows facing the front with curved rows of chairs? That way, worshippers can sense the presence of others in the space as well as focus on the altar.

In worship, visibility of leaders is particularly important. The vocalists and musicians need to be placed where they can easily be seen and heard. They should also contribute to the sense of gathering and not interfere with the focal point of the worship space.

Indeed, one of the critical decisions of worship planners is to decide on the focal point in the service. In most churches this actually involves no decision at all; everyone agrees with the architecture of the room that draws the vision to the table, the pulpit, the cross, or another significant symbol that stands at the "spiritual center." In alternate settings for worship, consider a strong, central focal point that is not dominated by a personality but rather a meaningful Christian symbol. The key point: Resist the temptation to place people and their technology at the focal point of the room for worship.

Creating a sense of sacred space is an important concept for everyone on your worship teams to understand. It is important to you because it is important to God. Just think back through all of the detail God gave his people for temple and tabernacle design and construction. God knows that when we come to worship, because God is Spirit, we can benefit from sensory reminders of God's presence and attributes. Let's be careful, then, about setting up any kind of confusion or discord in our worship spaces. Everything about the service should lead the eyes, the emotions, and the heart into the presence of God.

"Splendor and majesty are before him; strength and glory are in his sanctuary.

"Ascribe to the Lord, O families of nations, ascribe to the Lord glory and strength.

"Ascribe to the Lord the glory due his name; bring an offering and come into his courts.

"Worship the Lord in the splendor of his holiness; tremble before him, all the earth"

(PSALM 96:6-9).

Decide Who Holds What

What will we hold in our hands as we worship?

I suggest creating a bulletin and printing everything in it, including the music and text of all congregational songs (remember to get required permissions). Having everything there and in order will alleviate the need for worshippers to constantly flip pages and search through hymnals. This strategy is user-friendly, especially for visitors, and far less distracting. You might consider ruling against inserts of any kind (realizing that all rules invite an occasional exception).

An 11x17 piece of paper gives four 8½x11 pages, and should give you enough space to include both words and melody line for all the worship songs. Although not everyone reads music, anyone can look at notes and tell up from down. Bulletins with melody and text greatly enhance the ability of a congregation to sing. Also include an outline of the sermon, which encourages people to follow more closely, and suggest they jot some notes and then take the outline home for reference during the week. Encourage all worshippers to take bulletins and Tool Kits (packets of Christian-growth materials) home with them for use during the week.

We live in what some would call a biblically illiterate society. Most people aren't accustomed to looking up verses in a Bible or using it as a reference point for any part of life. Certainly, part of the work of the church and worship ought to be to teach people how to use the Bible.

The church should also be in the business of distributing Bibles to those who don't have them, and worship is the perfect time for this. Place Bibles throughout your worship space, and invite worshippers to turn to the passages in Scripture that are referred to during the service. Invite them to take the Bible home if they don't have one— or give it to a friend or neighbor who needs one.

Think Through the "Child Challenge"

We love them dearly, but children can be a challenge, too, as we seek to disciple them for the Lord. Sadly, the typical worship environment is anti-child with rules such as the following:

- Maintain silence.
- Don't move.
- Read the music—and appreciate it.
- Listen with interest to a talking head for thirty minutes.
- Keep your hands quiet and to yourself.
- No bathroom break for one hour.
- Don't stand on your chair, even if you're too short to see anything.
- And...*no toys provided!*

Are these rules good for our kids? It has become increasingly clear from a number of studies, that children who have no positive early church memories are less likely to be involved in church as adults. With family time at a premium and value systems eroding, where will families build a meaningful spiritual foundation for themselves? Children need the support of church, family, and community as they grow in faith. And the church must ensure its own future by nurturing whatever "family faith time" it can create.

So, the question arises, what are we going to do about it? Here are a few ideas to consider:

- In all public worship events, include a children's message that follows the sermon theme but is truly and honestly targeted to kids.
- Include children's songs in the services.
- Draw kids in with age-appropriate readings.
- Use children's choirs as worship leaders.
- Use kids in the worship teams, in front of the congregation, and leading worship with their families.
- Invite the church-school kids to lead the first ten minutes of worship several times a year.
- If certain grades of church school are studying worship, encourage them to plan and lead an entire worship experience.
- Create a kids' worship cart that contains children's bulletins, both for pre-readers and readers, bags of soft toys, and children's Bibles.
- Along with coffee and rolls for adults, serve lemonade and cookies for kids.
- Provide a cry room and/or a video-overflow room where people with small children can go and still stay connected with the service.
- Incorporate celebration events into the worship experience to mark milestone events for children and their families, such as celebration of baptism, learning the Lord's Prayer, taking first Communion, and receiving a first Bible. Such events will bring the family together in worship. And that's a good thing!

Get Tech Savvy—Now!

As the church moves toward its "ancient-future," it will learn to artfully combine new technologies with ancient symbols. On one hand, good worship should make for bad television; but on the other hand, technology can be reappropriated for conveying God's truth in new and creative ways.

So what's happening with video projection? Many churches are discovering the powerful impact of using video (and other visual technologies) within their worship services. PowerPoint presentations of sermon outlines; video images, maps, illustrations, film clips, and Web pages are all available as tools to clearly communicate the gospel when projected by a video projector. Check out what's available on www.preachingplus.com. Video projection technology has come down dramatically in price and is now feasible for almost any congregation wishing to use images or projected text in worship.

If video projection is in your future plans, you will want to consider installing motorized draperies or shades to control the amount of light coming into the worship space. Glass windows are beautiful until you want to project images. Drapery technology has advanced greatly in the last five years. Now, with the push of button, you can have your worship space change from bright sunlight to complete blackout, if necessary.

How effective are your lighting systems? Lighting can make or break a worship event, and your ability to control the light should not be taken...lightly. Generally, your lighting should promote a sense of joy in worship. It should create an aura of bright cheerfulness and make the space feel welcoming. It is especially important to highlight the altar. The lighting should also focus on people, banners, and whatever artistic statement is being made. The key is to have a capable person in charge and to make sure that your specific lighting needs at any moment in the service are quickly and easily met.

Do you really have "sound" sound? Excellent systems are an essential ingredient of new worship initiatives. When making decisions in this area, incorporate the input of a professional sound-system engineering firm, and seek the advice of an acoustical consultant. A sound system should reinforce all music and spoken word that occurs in your worship space and enhance the singing of the congregation. All spoken words should be clearly audible and pleasing. A sound system should draw a listener's ear to the focal point of the room. Sound should extend into church hallways, overflow spaces, the cry room, and bathrooms.

Check Out That View!

Why neglect the great outdoors? Outdoor worship has been part of our church's fabric since the summer of 1972. In an effort to reach out to those who might not come through the door of a typical church building, and as a way to encourage a more evangelistic mindset, we opted to begin outdoor services at a drive-in movie theatre. Worshippers would drive in, put the little metal boxes on their car windows, and worship in their cars. This new concept took off with the kind of success that we had never anticipated. After a single summer, hundreds of new people had come to see, hear, and experience the love of God in this unique setting.

Of course, there were many good and understandable reasons not to hold worship outdoors:

- What if it's too hot?
- What if it rains?
- Most people are gone in the summer anyway!
- You're going to haul all that stuff, set it up, tear it down, then haul it back to the church again, time after time?

There were also many good and understandable reasons to do it this way:

- People love being outside.
- People enjoy new ideas and unique experiences.
- Many who never attend church indoors find it comfortable to worship outdoors.

After three very successful years of drive-in worship, we decided to incorporate the outdoor worship concept into our new church site (mainly because of all the new people coming to us). Outdoor worship continues to be a unique and wonderful experience for all who attend. We've learned a lot in this journey, and here are some pointers.

• *Make it an awesome location.* First, choose a great site for people to gather outdoors. This may be next to a parking area where folks can still worship in their cars if they wish. It's OK if worship leaders face the sun, but you don't want a worshipping congregation facing the sun all morning.

No matter how you arrange your location, though, remember that you'll need a "distraction plan." Create a worship environment where all can see and hear. Minimize distractions among the worshippers first. Anticipate the occasional jet or truck that might disturb the proceedings. Just smile, wait, and let it pass. Anticipate the occasional siren. Stop and pray for those who might be in distress.

• *Make comfort and convenience the highest of priorities.* Encourage worshippers to bring blankets and lawn chairs. Provide comfortable folding chairs for those who come unprepared. Encourage people to bring their own coffee mugs, and then provide coffee, rolls, lemonade, and an informational table in a space near, but separate from, the worship space.

For distribution of print materials, create two ushers' stations to store and distribute printed materials for worship. Attach a tall flag to each so worshippers can see where they are and leaders can point them out. All bulletins, Tool Kits, and other printed materials can be distributed from these stations. The print materials should be printed on colored paper because it's impossible to read from white paper in bright sunshine. Enlarge the type as much as possible.

Remember that outdoor worship is a very child friendly environment. Provide the same kid cart that you have indoor for bulletins, soft toys, and Bibles. Finally, keep the service shorter than the indoor services. We've found that a thirty-five-minute service is ideal.

• *Make sure the weather won't ruin your day.* Yes, you'll need to plan for all kinds of weather. Constantly encourage worshippers to come prepared—use sunscreen; bring umbrellas; have raincoats handy. For your part, do things such as provide a shaded area for those who cannot tolerate direct sunlight.

Then…have a rain plan. In case of a rainout, where can you go and still have a worthwhile experience together? Also, have a wind plan. Purchase wind screens for your microphones and small sandbags to hold down the music stands and musical equipment. Buy Plexiglas plastic to cover music on the stands, and use deep offering baskets with covers. Communion wafers should be kept in weighted baskets. Use rocks or Plexiglas to cover the printed materials at the ushers' stations.

• *Make sound decisions—about sound.* Purchase a quality public address system with great monitors. In an outdoor environment, it's very difficult for musicians to hear each other. Good monitoring is critical. Have plenty of guitar tuners; sun and strings don't work well together.

• *Establish teams of helpers to set up and tear down.* To include car worshippers, use a limited-area broadcasting unit, such as those that broadcast to the headsets of exercisers in health clubs. These units cost about three hundred dollars and are readily available. You may need to modify the antennas to boost the signal to the cars.

Sound good? Try it!

CHECKPOINTS

1. In a group, think through the many "contact points" in your church. Brainstorm ways you could make each of them more inviting or hospitable.
2. Evaluate your "sense of gathering" according to the criteria given in this chapter. What are your specific strengths and weaknesses in this area?
3. What do people hold in their hands when they worship in your church? How are these things helping—or hindering—their experience of true worship?
4. Think through the ways your church handles the "child challenge." List some specific ways the children are benefiting and growing spiritually as a result.

5. Is your church "tech savvy"? If not, what's the first thing that needs to be changed?

6. What is your reaction to the idea of outdoor worship? How might you be able to make it happen in your setting?

SUMMARY POINTS

1. The worship space must provide a "sense of gathering," an environment that appreciates the gathered community and acknowledges its presence.

2. The focal point of worship space should be strong Christian symbols like an altar, cross, and font instead of people or technology.

3. Hospitality systems are critical to the worship experience from the parking lot to the pew, including the welcoming of children.

4. Lighting, video, and sound systems are important to the environment you want to create.

5. Outdoor worship may provide a great postmodern, child friendly option for seasonal worship.

CHAPTER 6

Putting It All Together—Like a Work of Art!

The artful construction and planning of worship is much like creating a great painting. The textures, colors, and hues of paint can be mixed and layered to achieve an amazing work of art. We first assemble all the tools necessary and then put in place all of the elements to create the artistry of worship.

This worship experience needs to remind us all of where we find ourselves in the great story. We aren't the first Christians to come along, and we won't be the last. We're linked to the Creation story, to the story of Israel, to the story of the first disciples, to our current story, and to the story of all that is to come until the end of time. Our worship needs to remind us of our place in God's history as we celebrate our Trinitarian heritage—giving glory to the Father, Son, and Holy Spirit.

At some point, a team of people must pick up the palette of colors and, with careful brush strokes, arrange all these elements in an artful way. I would suggest the following techniques for producing a beautiful worship experience in your congregation.

Make Use of Tactile Rituals

New (and old) tactile rituals are a great way to involve worshippers and add "embodied response" to the "canvas" of worship. Such rituals allow more than just one of the senses to come into play. (Normally churches engage hearing only.) Sometimes the creative use of metaphor demands a tactile ritual to give outward manifestation to an inward motivation. What do I mean? Consider the following ideas:

• **Reconciliation Rocks.** In a service of reconciliation we gave a large, flat rock to each worshipper as he or she entered. At the conclusion of the service, our pastor invited each person to give a name and a face to the rock. They were each to think of someone with whom he or she needed reconciliation, to think of the pain that was separating them from a loved one, or about the anger or guilt necessary to relinquish in order to move on. Worshippers were reminded that we can give all of these things back to God and leave them there.

Everyone was invited to come to the altar, place the rock in a basket, and…leave it. To us, it was an amazing experience to see and hear the rocks hit each other and to see people leaving the service having given bodily expression to all the hurt they'd been carrying inside. The rocks were then moved to a place in the landscaping and remain there today. Those rocks will be joined by others over the years as we continue to hold reconciliation services.

• **Prayer Cards.** In every worship service we make prayer cards available on which worshippers can write their concerns and requests and place them in the offering baskets. During the week, prayer teams will pray for these requests. Occasionally, we will invite everyone to write out a prayer concern on a prayer card and, in processional ritual, come to the altar and place the concern on the altar. In turn, they may take the prayer card of someone else and pray during the coming week. What an incredible joy it is for us to know that thousands of prayers are being prayed because this ritual connected people by their deepest needs.

• **Cross Nails.** During Lent we distributed large, black concrete nails that symbolized the nails used to crucify Christ. Each worshipper was invited to carry a nail throughout the season as a daily reminder of Christ's sacrifice. Many people carried the nails in their pockets or purses and told us what powerful reminders the nails were for them.

• **Covenants With God.** At the conclusion of a worship series based on the Marks of Discipleship, instead of using financial pledge forms, we gave worshippers the chance to respond to God as they were able. We invited worshippers to bring postage stamps with them on this particular weekend, and then distributed a covenant form regarding the Marks of Discipleship, together with envelopes and pencils. Everyone, including children, was invited to fill out the form or write a letter to God telling how he or she would respond to God's goodness during the coming year. We gave ample time and direction for them to fill out the forms, fold them, place them in the envelopes, address them to themselves, and place stamps on them. After a time of prayer and blessing, everyone was invited to bring the covenant form to the altar and give it to God. We made sure that worshippers understood that their covenants were between them and God and that no one would open their envelopes. We mailed the envelopes a month later as reminders of the covenants that the people had made with God during this ritual.

These are just four examples of the kinds of tactile rituals that can add "art" to worship and move it from a mere "come and see" event to a "come and experience" event.

Texture Your Technology

Technology is all around us in varied and multiple forms. The word is usually associated with electronics, but there are many other forms that, when *layered* (that's what I mean by *textured*) with projection, lighting, and sound systems can be powerful. Textured technology might include candles, leaded glass, crosses, fountains, running water, bread and wine, bells, and tapestries. We tend to view these elements as set apart from technology, but there is new power in the creative juxtaposition of old and new. The new technology can increase our focus on the old—the dynamic range between light and darkness, or the sensory nature of the act of worship.

In reality, we have a new opportunity to reclaim all of the arts within the worship environment. With God as the great giver of all inspiration, worship can be a celebration of creativity and inspiration. Drama, dance, sculpture, poetry, performance art, photography, and film can add to the creative expression that will help a worshipper experience the presence of God. Christianity and the Arts is a periodical that can be helpful in these discussions. It's available at www.christianarts.net.

Concentrate on Concentric Thinking

Most of us over forty tend to be linear thinkers. We naturally fall into a pattern of doing first one thing and then the next, and we prefer to do things in order. A growing percentage of the people sitting in your congregation are not wired that way. They are concentric thinkers. They are comfortable doing five or six things simultaneously, such as watching television, ironing or cleaning drawers, catching up on reading or mending, and cooking a meal. Anything short of that level of involvement is boring to them.

Good worship is really a series of action verbs. In worship we need to give our people enough to keep them involved and to engage all the senses. They can view banners or other visually attractive art forms; listen to spoken or musical interpretation; respond in writing; watch dance, drama, or video; or all of the above. Future worship planners will need to work in a multitude of communication modes. If your worship moves along with everyone doing one thing at a time, the experience may be less than stimulating to many.

Make a Script—and Stick to It!

A word for word script of each worship service should be created specifically for the pastors and worship leaders and distributed in plenty of time prior to the service. This "leader's guide" is scripted as completely as possible, right down to the announcements. All transitions are included, anticipating dead spaces, and pastors are strongly encouraged to stick to the script unless they can improve on it.

The key is to plan for any possible gaps in timing. Anticipate the transitions and create a plan to ensure that they are as seamless as possible. Provide each person in leadership with this scripted leader's guide. It also helps to involve more than one person in the service leadership and, for some of you, that means bringing other musicians into new roles or filling lay worship leading positions from your congregations. If that is the case, you will need to schedule practice times and involve a team of dependable assistants, just as you have with musicians.

Now a quick word about applause. Clapping can be a real distraction for some people, and we are generally intentional about discouraging it because it can lead us to the wrong conclusions regarding who is to be thanked within the worship environment. Clapping also tends to slow the pace of the worship events. Conversely, if each element of worship follows closely upon the one before, uncomfortable gaps are eliminated. Silence should be planned and enjoyed by all, not just experienced as the inadvertent gaps between elements in worship. On the other hand, spontaneous clapping is acceptable, natural, and something to celebrate on occasion.

Before concluding this book, I'd like to lay out for you a sample worship format based on the three-fold movement described on page 29—Welcome, Equip, and Send. This is obviously only a general plan, and you'll adapt it to your unique needs. Also, note that I've included all possible elements that could be used; however, you wouldn't use each of these in any one service. Rather, you would pick the appropriate worship events from under each of the three movements, depending on your needs in a particular service.

May God richly bless you and all who worship together in Jesus' name.

A Sample Worship Format

THE BULLETIN
(Provides the following written directions at top of first page.)

Please enjoy your refreshments before entering the sanctuary.

Bulletins and weeklies are available at each usher's station.

Children's bulletins, soft toys, and children's Bibles are available at the two children's stations in the back of the sanctuary.

Help us create a worship environment where all can see and hear by keeping movement and noise to a minimum. For those with small children who need more room to roam, the service is televised in the coffee area.

We encourage you to take your bulletin and weekly home with you and use them throughout the coming week.

If you have comments, questions, reactions, or responses to this worship service, please call the worship hotline at (555) 555-5555.

WELCOME
(This is the entrance portion of the three-fold pattern of worship. It may include the following:)

Gathering Music
(10 minutes of instrumental music.)

Invitation to Worship
(A verbal welcome and description of what we're going to do together.)

1. Welcome to worship! As you entered worship today, you received a "Tool Kit," which provides Christian-growth tools

for you to use throughout the coming week. Please look at page one of the Tool Kit, where you will find congregational announcements for the week ahead.

2. We also want you to notice the "People of Prayer" page, where you will find a listing of all the known prayer concerns of this congregation. We invite you to use this page as a prayer guide for your personal prayers during worship today and throughout the coming week.

3. If you turn the "People of Prayer" sheet over, you will find the "Bring It Home" devotional. This is a seven-day devotional reading for you to use throughout the coming week.

4. Worship is the activity of all God's people. We invite you to join in the singing of songs and responding as indicated in your bulletin.

5. Together we're exploring what it means to _____ again.

A Visual/Auditory Element
(It might be an art sketch, a metaphor, a film clip, a sound effect, a photo, or a newspaper article to focus us on the direction for our worship.)

The Call to Worship
(A verbal, responsive gathering statement, often based on the Old Testament reading for the day.)

Gathering Music
(A song, hymn, or medley to gather us as God's people into a framework and mindset for worship.)

Welcome to Worship
(Worshippers turn and greet each other.)

Leader: Good morning!

People: Good morning!

Leader: This is God's day, and we are the body of Christ gathered in Christian community. We invite you to spend the next minute moving about the worship area greeting one another, introducing yourselves, and saying "Good morning."

Distribution of Welcome Folders
(A folder including prayer dots, prayer cards, pen, and a sign-in form is given to the first worshipper in each row.)

Leader: At this time we are distributing our Welcome Folders so you can sign your name and check what may apply to you or your family. Pass the folder to the next person in your row, and after it reaches the end of the row, pass it back again. Also in the welcome folder are the prayer dots and prayer request cards.

We encourage you to take a green dot and place it on the face of your watch. Throughout the week, as you look at your watch, let the green dot serve as a reminder to pray for your church and the concerns we share as a community. If you have a specific prayer request, write it on the card, place it in the offering plate, and we will have our prayer teams praying for you this week.

EQUIP
(This is the "Word" portion of the three-fold pattern of worship. It may include the following:)

Scripture Reading(s)
(The readings for the day are read. The context for the readings is shared, along with brief, but interesting exegetical or historical information about the text. Worshippers open Bibles and turn to the passages.)

Leader: We invite you to take the Bible located in your chair. If you don't have a Bible, the one you hold in your hand is for you to take home with you. Or, if you know someone who doesn't have a Bible, take this Bible and give it to him or her as a gift.

Children's Song
(We sing a children's song as the children gather with the pastor for the children's message. This song ties directly to the texts and theme of the day.)

Children's Message
(The children's message speaks directly to the kids about the day's worship theme and how they can apply it. It is for the children— avoiding abstract language and ending in prayer with the kids.)

Children's Song
(We sing another portion of the children's song as the kids return to their seats.)

Message
(The sermon is preached at this point, with strong references back to the biblical texts. A fill-in-the-blank outline helps those who learn best this way. The message is supported with PowerPoint presentations of the outline, video clips, music, and other elements to enhance the impact.)

Response to the Message
(A contemplative, meditative musical response to what has been preached. Sometimes music selection might underscore the conclusion of the message. This element might be preplanned or spontaneous.)

Creed
(This depends on your denominational affiliation. This may be a historic statement, such as the Apostles' Creed or the Nicene Creed. Or you may have developed your own version of a Christian creed that also conveys the distinctives of your church's mission and focus.)

SEND

(This is the "sending" portion of the three-fold pattern of worship. It combines the "table" and "sending" portions of the four-fold pattern (see pages 28-29).

Offering

Leader: Now we join Christians all over the world in worshipping God through our giving. If you are a first-time worshipper, you are our guest, and we do not expect you to give an offering. For members and friends, the mission and ministry of this congregation is completely dependent upon your generous giving. Our offering is a significant act of worship.

As we worship God through our giving, we will also worship God in our singing.

Offering Music

(The congregation sings a thematically tied musical selection together as the offering is received.)

Prayer of Blessing

(The ushers bring the offering forward, and we pray a prayer of blessing for the use of these gifts that God has given.)

Confession/Forgiveness

(In preparation for Communion, we enter into a time of confessing sins and seeking forgiveness. This varies from a completely scripted responsive form to prayers of confession prayed freely by pastors and others. The pastor declares the forgiveness of sins based on 1 John 1:9-13.)

Communion Litany

(This is for services in which Communion will be observed. We are welcomed to the table with words that remind us of our place in God's history and of God's saving action on our behalf in Jesus Christ.)

Words of Institution

(We hear the words of Jesus regarding the Lord's Supper.)

Prayers
(We welcome the presence of the Holy Spirit to come among us in the meal.)

Lord's Prayer
(We pray the prayer Christ taught us to pray.)

Communion Notes
(You may place in your bulletin notes like those below, depending on how your church observes Communion.)

1. We invite the Communion servers, musicians, and ushers to come and commune as we give instructions.

2. All are invited to come and receive the cup and bread.

3. The ushers will direct you from your rows toward the center aisle. Come forward to the serving stations. If you desire to commune, extend your hand to the server, who will place a wafer in your hand. Touch the wafer to the wine or the white-colored grape juice in the split chalice, and then eat the elements. Children will receive a blessing.

4. If you would like to kneel at the altar railing for a time of personal prayer and reflection, we invite you to do so after you have communed.

5. Please return to your seats by the side aisle.

6. As we commune, we sing of the life, death, and resurrection of Jesus Christ. Join us in singing as we commune together. Come and hold in your hand and taste on your lips the love which we cannot comprehend.

COMMUNION DISTRIBUTION

Communion Music
(Songs and hymns are sung together as we take Communion. Prayer partners are at the altar rail to pray privately with individuals.)

Song of Thanksgiving

(A congregational hymn or song that reiterates the worship theme and its call for response.)

Benediction

(A benediction that ties into the worship theme of the day.)

Sending Music

(Instrumental music sends worshippers out to serve in Jesus' name.)

Evaluating Your Services

It is critical to implement a systematic evaluation process to allow everyone to express concerns and questions. Evaluation is a healthy way to plan for the future as long as you take care to follow a systematic approach.

Good evaluation should emphasize the ministry and de-emphasize the individuals involved. We need to be able to *objectively* assess each other's participation in worship. Emphasis on quality and dedication to the vision for ministry, combined with a sincere respect for the integrity of each servant of God, will go a long way toward ensuring positive results.

Finally, establish a worship hotline that invites every worshipper to call with their concerns and questions. Occasionally, use a written evaluation form in the Tool Kit to assess the particular value of a given worship experience. Staff evaluation is on-going and occurs in a multitude of ways. Here is a sample form you can adapt for your own use.

How did we do today?

Please tear this off and place it in the offering plate.

SERMON	poor	fair	good	great
MUSIC	poor	fair	good	great
FACILITIES	poor	fair	good	great
PARKING	poor	fair	good	great
COMMUNICATION	poor	fair	good	great

Comments_____

_____

Service Time_____Date_____
Name_____

CHECKPOINTS

1. How would you define "tactile ritual"? What ideas do you have for implementing such experiences in your worship services?

2. What is your reaction to the idea of targeting your worship to concentric thinkers?

3. Which ideas given in the sample worship service would you like to try in your church? How do you think these would work? Why?

4. What types of evaluation processes do you have in place? If there are none, would you consider using the sample Evaluation Form above? Why or why not?

SUMMARY POINTS

1. The worship planning palette combines artistic elements to paint a worship environment where a worshipper can experience the presence of God.

2. Worship art considers the historical place of the present assembly and the Trinitarian nature of worship.

3. Tactile rituals extend the possibilities of worship to include experiential elements.

4. The worship arts environment should interface technology with textured elements within the space.

5. All art and language combine to create a concentric experience of the presence of God.